10/29/2020

Dear Donavan,

On a cool night in 1975, your angels guarded you from the car that plowed into your home and stopped just short of your crib! That night also started the friendship between your family and mine! Thank you for being a catalyst at the risk of your life :)

Love & hugs,
Pam

How to Help *Yourself* to Be Who You *Want to Be*

A Simple Guide for Those Who Are Ready to Take Charge and Redirect Their Lives

Pam Grewall

HOW TO HELP YOURSELF TO BE WHO YOU WANT TO BE
A SIMPLE GUIDE FOR THOSE WHO ARE READY TO
TAKE CHARGE AND REDIRECT THEIR LIVES

iUniverse books may be ordered through booksellers or by contacting:

iUniverse
1663 Liberty Drive
Bloomington, IN 47403
www.iuniverse.com
844-349-9409

ISBN: 978-1-5320-9403-3 (sc)
ISBN: 978-1-5320-9401-9 (hc)
ISBN: 978-1-5320-9402-6 (e)

Library of Congress Control Number: 2020917009

Print information available on the last page.

iUniverse rev. date: 10/12/2020

To all who wish to learn and make better lives for themselves; all who have at one time or another questioned their worth; all who are on missions to become masters of their destinies; all who have felt overwhelmed by the monumental tasks ahead; and all who have wished to find a simpler way to tackle them.

Help yourself! Become a cocreator of your personality, your character, and your destiny. Understand what to do. Learn how to do it in easy-to-follow steps.

- Set goals.
- Learn from the past.
- Plan for the future.
- But live life—one day at a time—in the present.

Acknowledgments

Although everyone who has crossed paths with me, traveled some distance with me, or stayed with me has influenced me and contributed greatly to who I am today, I would like to specially acknowledge the roles the following people have played in my experiences leading up to my writing this book.

My family, friends, and even those not very friendly, thank you for my experiences—both positive and negative. Being with you all has taught me to be grateful for what I have and enabled me to rise above situations to become a woman of strength instead of remaining a victim. Special thanks to my father, who nurtured my interest in spiritual pursuits and self-help tools. Heartfelt gratitude to my mother for her immense love for humanity, which taught me to embrace all as my human family. Her generously loving heart showed me that the more you give of yourself and share your bounty, the more you receive from the universe. The unshakeable faith of both my parents gave me the stability to weather many a storm and come out ahead.

Many thanks to my children, who have been great teachers and who always challenged me to be a better version of myself to set a good example for them.

I thank my friend Carol Owens, who years ago planted the seed by suggesting that I consider coaching or counseling because she thought I had a unique way of getting to the heart of the matter. Although it took many years before I got to that point, that comment stayed buried in my subconscious until an astrologer in India asked me why I wasn't writing a book. By then, I felt that what I had to say had been said over and over again. She then told me that *how* I say it is unique, reminding me once again of Carol's comment.

I offer thanks to Sister Sophia, who came into my life at a very vulnerable time, helped me wade through troubled waters, and then just as mysteriously faded out of my life. I have shared some stories of meeting her and how she helped me. Wherever you are now, I thank you from the bottom of my heart.

Thanks also to Gary Quinn, author, life coach, and teacher. My angels guided me to your book signing and then to becoming a certified life coach with you. Your books have helped me to work through blocks, reach for the stars, and believe that I am capable of and worthy of whatever I choose to do and however high I wish to fly.

Suzie Emiliozzi, thank you for your gentle guidance and help in removing blocks, negativity, guilt, and anger that were hiding in my subconscious from many lifetimes and for many generations. This has allowed creativity to flow through again and has cleared the path and lightened my load by releasing memories and emotions that no longer served me.

iUniverse publishing, editorial and design teams, thank you for your persistence in following up on my tentative query about self-publishing and your infinite patience in answering my questions. Thank you also for your invaluable input and gentle prodding without pushing. Your prompt responses, knowledgeable input, and wise guidance have helped me immensely in determining my course of action.

A very special thank-you goes out to Monte Richter for juggling her very busy schedule and giving me her feedback.

I am grateful for access to unlimited knowledge through media, books, and magazines. Thank you to all the authors, present and past, who reached out with answers through the pages of their writings when I had questions. Thank you to everyone, who it would be impossible to name, for enabling me to put together this work to share my knowledge and pay it forward.

Introduction

There is only one thing more painful than learning from
experience and that is not learning from experience.
—Archibald MacLeish

Are you ready to embark on this journey to a new you? This book is
a simple manual that will help you recognize your strengths and
weaknesses and understand that you're the maker of your destiny. Even
though simple may not be easy, it will still be worth the effort you put into
it. Recognizing where you left your authentic self behind, and recovering
it, will be unbelievably empowering.

This book is a signpost or guide to point the way. It offers suggestions
and resources for you to decide what is the best course for you, thus
encouraging you to understand yourself, know yourself, and based on
that, take action. Its purpose is for you to empower yourself by taking
back the power that, at some point in your life, you relinquished and thus
became a victim. But now you're ready to be a victim no more. It points
the way, but the journey must be yours.

This book is meant to be a conversation starter, an overview, including
various topics or situations. If you're experiencing any of these issues
or situations mentioned here, by addressing these, you could bring big
changes to your life. But if you ignore them and simply hope that they
will go away if you don't pay any attention, these will become part of your
subconscious. You won't consciously be aware of them after some time,
but they will become triggers for your responses and actions and may
even sabotage you.

It's usually uncomfortable to talk about them with friends and family. We want to appear perfect in the eyes of our mates, children, or the other people in our lives. Somehow, having any of these problems means we're imperfect, and we feel inadequate, insecure, or vulnerable. Realizing that it's a journey toward perfection and it's okay to be imperfect while we move forward is a victory and a big step in the right direction. If you lived in a fortress with massive walls that no one could break or penetrate, you would feel safe. However, if that fortress had a weak spot or a hole in the wall that anyone could come through, it would be in your best interest to become aware of that and guard it well until it could be repaired, or you would be just as vulnerable as if you weren't secured at all. Similarly, our faults and imperfections, when acknowledged, recognized, and addressed can become our greatest strengths.

Life experience and self-learning shouldn't be invalidated just because a degree isn't conferred upon you by a recognized institution. There are many cases of people paying for these degrees rather than earning them through genuine learning. Accept learning and wisdom from sources that are genuine and that help you grow even if they don't have those validating letters after their names. Remember: learning often happens outside the classroom in the school of life. Even the most prestigious schools began with such learning before developing a standardized curriculum.

While the topics in this book are important and vast enough to justify a whole book for each one, it is important to deal with one step at a time so you don't get buried in everything at once.

The book incorporates views, opinions, observations, experiences, and lessons gleaned over a lifetime. These are my opinions based on my understanding of life. Someone once asked, "How do you eat an elephant?" And the response was, "One bite at a time." Obviously, this wasn't really about eating an elephant, but it was a great analogy for tackling a monumental task. We complete it by tackling one step at a time instead of trying to deal with the whole. With that understanding, I've tried to interpret the vast panorama of human existence and our connection to the universe by breaking it down to small "bites" to make it "digestible."

Every speck incorporates the entire process on a smaller scale. So, instead of being overwhelmed by its vastness, even though I'm in awe of its endlessness, I view it on a smaller scale to simplify it for my limited understanding to comprehend it and find my place in it. Doing that gave me a purpose and the knowledge that I'm not merely a "free radical" floating aimlessly in the cosmos. It helped me realize that no matter how small my contribution to the whole, it is nonetheless essential. A nail in a building may seem insignificant, but it's essential to hold something in place that is supporting the building. So, even though the subject matter may seem to be vast, and at times unrelated, however, parts of it will resonate with everyone. I've used symbolism and analogies from everyday life to drive home certain points. I find that this helps me to retain the message and learn the lesson more easily, so I hope you'll find it helpful also.

As the dynamics of life change, so must the rules that we live life by. With all the technological advances, our reach has become more global rather than just local, more instant than time lapsing. Right now, life is like a roller coaster going at full speed, and one must be securely belted in if one isn't to fall off. The ride slows down and stops briefly to drop off current riders and pick up new ones. Once that's done and seat belts are fastened, it takes off again. We each have one ride and then must get off. Once it stops, we can go to the end of the line to start over if we want to ride it again, but we can't just stay on endlessly while others are waiting. It's imperative that we take all the necessary precautions to make it a safe ride and follow the rules, such as not sticking our arms or legs out to endanger ourselves and others. For those seeking more thrills, they must find other rides that will allow them to do that.

Similarly, living life constructively and making a difference, facilitating soul growth, and forming relationships requires us to take the necessary precautions and follow rules. Universal laws, such as the planets moving in their orbits, nature following its course and changing seasons, and days following nights and nights following days, are permanent and *always* apply. (Yes, there are laws that govern the operating of the universe. It isn't as random as it seems sometimes.) Souls on their journeys generating or repaying karmic debts by their actions and the choices they make, facilitating growth, and fulfilling their missions are all part of the universal laws that govern our existence. Human rules and laws are subject to current conditions and serve only for the length of time that the conditions remain the same. Once those change, these rules and laws become obsolete and must be revisited, revised, and modified. For example, the traffic rules that were applicable in the seventeenth and eighteenth centuries, when horses and buggies on dirt roads were the mode of transportation, are obsolete now with (for the most part) paved roads and fast vehicles.

This book is my attempt to hold a mirror to the current view, keep what's still valid, and discard that which no longer works to replace it with what does. As in a garden, it's necessary to remove weeds, dead blooms, dead leaves, and such so it continues to grow and be vibrant and colorful, fruitful and joyful instead of being buried under decayed and decomposing leaves and branches.

The best way to use this book is to read it through once, mark what you connect with, learn what may be new to you or what sparks your curiosity, and ignore what seems outlandish or mere fantasy that you may disagree with. These are my subjective experiences and lessons that you don't have to accept or agree with. It's as if you were to pick and choose what to order from a menu—mix and match, make the meal your own, and ignore the rest. Once you receive the food, you proceed to enjoy the meal. Sometimes, you choose foods you've tried and know that you like, or you choose comfort foods. Other times, you may feel curious and adventurous, so you try new items on the menu that your friends suggested. Then you save that as a good or bad experience. This is the fun of learning from other people's experiences.

In addition, when trying new dishes, you may like a particular dish, but you may not like certain ingredients in that dish, or you may want more or less of some other ingredients. If you like it, you may search for recipes and try to prepare it at home. You may tweak quantities, add or remove certain ingredients, and modify it to your taste while keeping the basic recipe.

When you're preparing a meal, you gather the ingredients that the recipe dictates. It's amazing how one can prepare dishes that look and taste totally different by using the same ingredients but simply changing the quantities, the method of cooking (baking, broiling, sautéing, or boiling), the length of time, or the order of adding the ingredients. Similarly, from the "ingredients," a.k.a. experiences of life, I have gleaned the best as I saw them and tossed them together to prepare a "new dish" with "old ingredients." There is no such thing as new information, as someone or other has said it sometime or other. All we can do is assemble information in a new way that makes sense to us based on what we know now.

Books are best used in a similar manner. You may connect with it as is, or you pick and choose what you connect with and want to incorporate in your life and your experiences, experiment with some other concepts, and learn more about them. Or yet again, you can totally ignore and move past to some other parts.

There's so much information available now on the internet on every subject, often contradictory but sometimes validating certain points of view, that the whole experience of researching it can be overwhelming.

As you read through quotes, thoughts, comments, essays, fables, stories, or poems, see what you connect with or what touches you based on your life experiences and take that and add it to your collection to use as a mirror to reflect, a cane to support, or a thorn to remove. Let the rest go. As in the supermarket, there are so many different items for sale, but you only pick up what you need now. All are useful but not necessarily what you need now. Of course, you may go back later for what you may need at another time in the future. Similarly, with this book, what isn't in your circle of experience today may become useful later. Revisit periodically to glean this information and incorporate that in your life.

Knowledge gives you power, but wisdom teaches you how to use that power. Glean the knowledge from many sources but don't drown in it. It's said that a little knowledge is a dangerous thing. It's good to have an overview of many topics and subjects, but to benefit from it, learn from it or own it, your knowledge needs to be deeper rather than wider. You can swim on the surface of the ocean and connect with some life forms, but to know and experience the majesty of its vast resources, one needs to dive into its depths. Allow yourself the time to ripen your knowledge into wisdom and a deeper understanding to fully reap its rewards.

When you do that, you'll be able to respond, not react. You'll also realize that the more you learn, the less you know. A child's universe is limited to his home, his parents, and immediate surroundings, but as he grows, he learns that there's a bigger world out there that he doesn't know but that's fun to explore. As time goes by, he finds that there's so much more to learn. He also realizes that he can't know everything. In school, he learns a little bit about many subjects. This helps him to decide what interests him more, so he picks what he wants to study in college. As he advances even more, he narrows down his choice to one subject for his master's degree. Then if he wants, he chooses to specialize in one more subject matter, getting a double master's or moves on to get a PhD. As he puts these to use in his work to earn a living, he continues to gain experience beyond just the book learning.

So, after reading the book, you'll find that you will perceive life from a different perspective and that it will either validate and add to what you already know or teach you something new. So, dear reader, sit back, relax, read and enjoy, incorporate, or ignore as you will.

If this book helps even one person rethink his or her destructive choices, change his or her negative direction to a more constructive path, or avoid a pitfall, the time and effort in writing this book will have been worth it. Life is a journey, and it's made pleasant or unpleasant by the companions or paths we choose. So, my friend, thank you for choosing to read the ramblings of my heart and have me as your companion on your journey!

> Note: The views and opinions expressed and the course of actions suggested are those of the author. No claim is made to imply that this is the only way. Readers should question, accept or reject as their own experiences dictate.

PART 1

What to Do

In this section, I've tried to address some of the issues that may be holding you back. Through essays, fables, stories, and quotes, I've attempted to show what blocks to look for. Knowing what's keeping you from living the best life you can is the first step to learning what you need to do to change the course of your life.

These are easy to comprehend but often difficult to implement. Our egos and minds are unwilling to let go of the control they exercise. They keep us locked in our stories and hurts—real or perceived. What we need to do is first find ways to appease them, sidestep them, and free ourselves from their grips to bring balance in our lives. They are both very important for survival, but they aren't the masters they claim to be. They must be reminded that our hearts and brains need equal space and time!

Conflict of Emotions Expressed and Repressed

A Painting by Jagvir Grewall

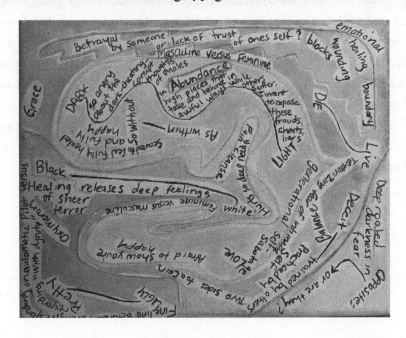

About the Painting

I drew this when I felt I couldn't breathe. I was suffocating from repressed and unexpressed emotions and feelings. I didn't know where these negative and hurtful thoughts were coming from, and I was so ashamed to be thinking such harsh and angry thoughts about some of the people I loved dearly. I decided to write those down so I could analyze and understand. When I was done writing these in pencil (I was going to erase these once I was done), I felt this image could help guide someone else to tackle the same issues, so I'm sharing it here in this book.

As I started to color the image, I realized that what I had drawn and the colors I had chosen actually looked like the lungs—exactly where I was feeling the blockage. (Even though I colored it, the black-and-white image somehow reflects the deep sadness as intensely as I was feeling it.) This helped me release a lot of deep-rooted emotions and memories in my subconscious that were triggering my insecurities and making me question my self-worth even though everyone looking at me told me I seemed to be a poised, self-confident, and beautiful young woman.

I realized these subconscious triggers went back many generations and many lifetimes. They were so deep-rooted and so old that I was consciously unaware of them even though they triggered a lot of my current reactions and responses. I was fortunate to find an energy worker who helped me release baggage that I was carrying even though it no longer served me.

I hope this helps you to unlock your emotions and set you free from whatever is keeping you imprisoned in yourself by self-sabotaging your efforts to break free.

Essays

The essays have been written in very simple words, and solutions may at times seem almost too simplistic. These are meant to serve as triggers to get started on helping yourself. In today's culture of internet learning, I felt the short essays and stories would be more effective. The purpose is to reduce what seem like overwhelming obstacles to bite-size pieces for better understanding and easier handling. Life isn't always this easy, but by changing our perception and tackling our problems in small portions, we can conquer situations that would otherwise seem insurmountable. It's okay not to deal with everything at the same time. Picking and choosing to prioritize doesn't imply that we're being blind to our reality. It simply means we're opening one window at a time. If we tried to access all the information in the computer at the same time and open too many windows, it would crash from the memory being overloaded. However, we can access all the information in smaller segments by opening a few windows at a time and, when done, moving on to the next lot.

The purpose of this book is to motivate you to help yourself rather than looking to others to do it for you. Understanding the process, being patient with yourself but staying consistent, will inspire you to make healthy and constructive choices instead of merely popping pills to take care of the symptoms. Pills help you bridge the gap while you're learning and changing course but reflection, understanding, and corrective actions will prevent you from becoming dependent on those pills.

At the end of each essay, there are some questions you can ask yourself and a section for your notes. This will help you reflect on your answers and will be truly helpful if you answer these honestly. Remember you're doing this to help elevate yourself and become a better human being. No one is judging you, so have no fear and set aside your ego. If you're able to do that and face yourself, you'll find a new strength in yourself. You'll then be able to face the world with a totally different perspective. Remember that true modesty is knowing your real worth. So, without an inflated ego or a deflated sense of self-worth, you'll know who you are and who you can be and still be okay with the fact that you're worthy now even though you can be worth a lot more in the future.

Controlling Anger

Anger is one letter short of danger.

—Unknown

There are positive emotions and negative emotions. All emotions also have both negative and positive aspects. They're essential to our being and express the state of our feelings. However, at the same time they also reflect the state of our thoughts. They can show whether we're secure or insecure, negative or positive, disciplined or not. They also affect the physical state of our being. Hence, it's imperative that we understand and take charge of our thoughts, feelings, emotions, and their expressions by learning to not react but to respond with enough force to convey the message but not so much force that we appear to be attacking or even actually attacking.

Feeling anger is very important because you as a human being react to what you perceive as an unfair or unjustified situation. If you don't become angry when you see a helpless child or an animal being treated cruelly, you wouldn't be alive to the sensibility of the necessity to respect all life. You will feel indignant that some unethical person is misusing his power to cause hurt or harm to those weaker than himself.

On the positive side, this emotion can motivate you to take action and rise up to help and protect the meek and the weak, but on the negative side, it can become very destructive and lead to uncontrolled, violent reactions. It's perfectly okay to be angry. It isn't a good idea to repress emotions.

However, it's still important to remember that anger is a powerful emotion and should be expressed responsibly. Respond, don't react. Acknowledge your anger. Step away for some time to determine the following:

Are you angry with the right person? Who are you angry with? Don't lash out indiscriminately at everyone who crosses your path or beat yourself up for being vulnerable. You're not responsible for other people's actions, but you're certainly responsible for your own responses.

Why are you angry? Are you angry for the right reasons? Is it because someone else didn't do right, or are you simply in a bad mood? Are you angry in response to rude or unacceptable behavior, actions, or statements and comments?

Are you angry to the right degree? Determine how much anger is justified. If something was said in the heat of the moment and the person apologized for it, let it go. If it happens frequently, address it calmly and let the person know that it's no longer acceptable. If it continues, don't keep placing yourself in the same circumstances again and again. If you continue to do so, know that you're not a victim but a facilitator. You're allowing the other person to treat you badly, so your anger against that person wouldn't be justified. It isn't always easy to walk away, as there can be mitigating circumstances. Make informed choices because you're now a participant. You're not responsible for the other person's behavior just as he or she isn't accountable for your angry reactions.

Your choices, responses, and actions will either empower you or enslave you. The anger and resulting frustration will keep festering so that, the next time something triggers it, you'll no longer be in control, because you've handed your thinking over to your reactions, and you're now being controlled by them.

If you wish to be free from this behavior, you'll need to do some honest soul-searching to dig deep and go back to the point where this started. Then you can start letting go by forgiving yourself for hurting others in your ignorance while forgiving others who hurt you in their ignorance. Forgiving doesn't mean people weren't wronged. It simply means that, in our ignorance, we act or react in hurtful ways, but now having become aware of the consequences of those actions, we're willing to change our behavior.

Using anger properly is the key to transforming behavior from destructive to constructive. It allows the emotion to release negative feelings, defuse the pressure, and see beyond seeking immediate satisfaction in a violent manner. We're all human, and there are times when we'll get angry. With a little monitoring and insight into our actions, we can circumvent becoming human bombs just waiting to explode.

Just as a flooded river can't be contained with flimsy boundaries, suppressed anger won't be contained. It will burst through when triggered by the smallest provocation from others. Then it becomes impossible to express it responsibly—with the right person, to the right degree. It explodes like a bomb with a short fuse. It ruins relationships. Angry people blame others for unleashing their anger, causing them to behave like a charging bull that you can't reason with. Blaming others for unleashing your anger isn't the solution.

Managing your anger well is the goal here. If you frequently lash out at others, think back on what your triggers were. Seek help and accept guidance. Most of all, accept responsibility and take action to correct that behavior.

EXERCISE

Write down answers to the following questions honestly and reflect on the answers so you can determine the actions you can take to free yourself. Honest self-reflection is key to finding where the root cause lies. This is the only way to heal yourself. Unless you acknowledge your anger, you'll continue to seek answers in others while the problem stays with you.

1. How do you handle anger? Do you express it or repress it?
2. If you repress it, do you have violent outbursts periodically?
3. Who or what triggers these violent outbursts?

4. How do you feel when you lash out?
5. Do you apologize to the person you lash out at, or do you try to justify your anger and place the blame on the other person for your behavior?
6. When you come to terms with you repressed anger issues, how can you learn to express it more responsibly?
7. If you express your anger in a more responsible manner, do you feel that it gets your message across more effectively?
8. Do you believe that addressing issues that make you angry helps you to heal relationships with less undercurrents?
9. When you feel uncontrollable anger but later either regret your actions, justify your behavior, or blame others for triggering your anger, have you considered that this could be due to chemical changes in the body due to nutritional deficiencies?
10. Are these incidents due to alcohol or substance abuse?

REMINDER

- Anger is a valid emotion.
- It's okay to be angry.
- Anger shouldn't be repressed but should be expressed responsibly. Once you get to the root of the problem, be sure to monitor your choices, so it doesn't build up again.
- Until you hold yourself accountable to yourself for your actions, you'll continue to get the same results. Only you can take actions to bring about the change that will move you forward to a better place where you're in charge of your behavior.

Notes

Notes

Dealing with Fear and Bullies

Do not fear mistakes. You will know failure. Continue to reach out.

—Benjamin Franklin

Success is not final, failure is not fatal: it is the courage to continue that counts.

—Winston Churchill

A bully is playing a game, one that he or she enjoys and needs. You're welcome to play this game if it makes you happy, but for most people, it will make you miserable.

—Seth Godin

We're often imprisoned by our own fears, such as fear of failure or fear of getting hurt. We often refuse to try something new in case we fail at it or don't like it. First of all, we'll never know that if we don't try it. If we do try it and don't like it, we can choose not to do it again. But think about this: if we do like it, we would have missed the opportunity to incorporate it into our lives. How bleak our lives would be if we failed to take a chance on love out of fear. It doesn't guarantee that we won't fail or get hurt, but, oh, the exhilaration we feel when we succeed far outweighs any fear we may have felt in expressing it.

Caution and fear aren't the same and shouldn't be used interchangeably. Being cautious is essential to survival. Indiscriminate daring and foolish risk taking doesn't mean lack of fear. In fact, most dares hide behind fear of not being accepted or of being seen as a coward.

When we hide behind our fear, we cower and make unwise choices, placing us in even worse situations. This has us showing false bravado and making foolish decisions to save face. It's more courageous to acknowledge our fear of being rejected, of being unpopular, but making right choices anyway, even if they're unpopular. When we stand up to our fears, we stop being victims or becoming targets of bullies. Bullies are simply people who play on other people's weaknesses—of which we all have many—and hiding behind their own fears of being outdone by others.

Imagine that you're in a fortress, protected by a high wall around. This wall is so high that few can scale it. It's fortified with bricks and cement so it can't be broken easily. Make sure that there's a door that you can open when you want to come out, or you will be imprisoned behind the very walls you have erected to protect you.

Examine these walls periodically to make sure there are no weak spots for someone to break through. If you do find any such weak spots, be sure to guard those well and don't ignore them. By doing so, you'll turn your weakness into strength. On the other hand, if you ignore or choose to not acknowledge your weaknesses, you'll make yourself vulnerable to attacks from others.

Having weaknesses doesn't make you weak. Not recognizing those weaknesses or ignoring them does. Acknowledging them and guarding yourself well gives you the extra strength to withstand any onslaughts by others. Often when we find some weakness in ourselves, we get so busy trying to cover it up or denying it that we leave ourselves more vulnerable for unethical people to use it against us by threatening to expose us. By stepping up and admitting our weak points, we no longer allow the others to hold that threat over us.

What should you do if you encounter hatred and bullying? If you have learned to love yourself, you won't buy into what the bullies are trying to sell—that you're weak and unlovable as you are. If you already believe that, then you just validate what the bullies are telling you.

When I was in fourth grade, the most popular girl in the class was miffed at me because I wouldn't follow her. I was new to the school and shy, so I didn't have too many friends. She asked all the girls to stop talking to me or playing with me. Everyone followed her except one girl who stood by me as the others played during recess. I chose to disregard her bullying because I believed in myself. Yes, it hurt, and of course, I was grateful to my new friend who stood by me. Now, years later, I don't know where that friend is, but whenever I think of her, I silently offer a prayer for her well-being and send her love and best wishes.

Know that generally bullies work in groups because they are insecure themselves, so they find strength in numbers.

Also know that it's okay not to follow the crowd. However, be wise and don't place yourself in danger by taking them on by yourself. Think back to see a pattern in what kind of personalities they pick on. They find the most vulnerable, lonely people who are afraid of offending others or who are convinced that they aren't good enough. They seldom pick on people who are confident and who believe in themselves. Being confident, lovable, and believing in yourself doesn't mean you're perfect. It simply means that you know that, like everyone else, you have faults and that sometimes you fail in your attempts, but you still keep trying, and you're not afraid to acknowledge that it's part of the learning process. You will fail sometimes. You won't be good at everything or even a few things sometimes, and that's okay. This is a very important step of changing the dynamics of the "helpless victim" that you may perceive yourself to be and become that self-confident person that the bullies can't invoke fear in.

Now, this doesn't mean that you should stop trying to become better or more proficient. This is just where you are at this moment in your life. This isn't the goal of your journey. If you can't be a tree, focus on being the best shrub that you can be. We all have different talents, and each one of us makes an important contribution to the whole. Yes, this means that even the bullies contribute in helping you improve yourself. You have a choice to either remain a victim and continue to bully yourself or step up and say, "This isn't who I am, and I won't believe their negative opinion of me."

So, if you shouldn't believe another person's opinion of you because it's negative, should you do the same if it's positive? After all, it's still someone else's opinion. That's true to the extent that if you have not assessed your strengths and weaknesses objectively and are always looking to others to validate you, you'll continue to be affected by them, becoming overconfident when they praise you and disappointed when they criticize you. It's important to find a balance. As human beings, we live in society, and the opinions of others do matter, but these shouldn't direct your life and validate or invalidate you as a person. Just use these as guidelines to stay on course. Praise from our parents, teachers, or peers motivates us to keep doing better. Constructive criticism from the same people helps us catch ourselves when we're veering off course.

Believe in yourself enough to recognize when these come from a genuine desire to help you. Be humble enough to know when someone is merely flattering you to build your ego for his or her own gain. Be smart enough to find the balance.

EXERCISE

Writing down honest answers to the following questions will help you to identify what fears are holding you hostage. It will also give you clarity on how to be free. Ask yourself these questions.

1. Why am I afraid to try new things?
2. If I feel I'm being bullied, what is it triggering in me that I need to look at? What is it that I'm not seeing?
3. How can I learn to get past my fear of the unknown?
4. Do I seek support when I need help, or do I perceive that as a sign of weakness?

REMINDER

- Failing at something doesn't make you a failure.
- When you fail on the road to success, it will only make you stronger and motivate you to try again, if you don't perceive it as a weakness but learn from it.
- Understanding why bullies do what they do will make it easier for you to forgive them, stop being a victim, and move forward.

Notes

Notes

Notes

Learning and Growing

Anyone who stops learning is old, whether at twenty or eighty.

—Henry Ford

How we learn, what we learn, and how much we learn is determined by our ability and willingness to open our minds to absorb new knowledge. Knowledge and wisdom are all around us, but we only absorb what we're capable of accepting, incorporating, and storing.

In an ocean, there are various types of fish, sponges, pieces of wood, rocks, metal, and so on. Each of these interact with, absorb, or use the water and nutrients in it in very different manners, just as there are different kinds of people in the world who absorb knowledge differently.

The fish eat, drink, live, breathe, and swim in the ocean. This is their whole existence. They can't live without it.

The sponges attach themselves to rocks and, when safely anchored, sway with the movement of the water while absorbing the nutrients.

Pieces of wood simply float if light enough and let the waves move them closer to shore, either returning with the wave or simply drifting onto the sand. Larger pieces of wood, like large logs, absorb water and sink in, but smaller and lighter pieces head for shore and dry up until the strong wind blows them into the water again or the high tide reclaims them. Then they float until they are either carried in or thrown out again.

Rocks, being heavier and more solid, take much longer to be polished or broken into smaller pieces as the waves pound against the shore and slowly but surely wear these rocks down. Rocks don't absorb the water but are shaped by external force and repetitive movement.

Metals sink down to the bottom of the ocean and, being in the water constantly, begin to rust and have algae or other plants grow around them, as they don't absorb any water, even though now they are surrounded by it.

Like the water, knowledge and wisdom surround us. We only accept and absorb as much as we're capable of. Each one of us absorbs and processes knowledge differently. Even in the same class, with the same teacher, every student learns and expresses information very differently. How that happens depends on our personalities and how open or closed our minds are. As human beings, we have the consciousness and awareness to choose differently, but often we don't recognize the inherent power within us. We, in our limited understanding, think we're incapable of changing. Often, we even refuse to change because we fear the unknown, but get comfortable in the niche we've carved for ourselves.

The laws that operate the universe mandate that eventually we must all grow spiritually, but we all grow at different rates. So even though it may seem frustrating to see people stuck in certain situations, we need to realize that unless they're ready to incorporate or accept the change, we can't force them to. Our purpose is to work on our own growth. While it's noble to help others—and by all means, we should lend a helping hand if someone has fallen and is trying to get up—we should recognize that if they aren't yet ready to move from there, we shouldn't drag them. Letting people absorb knowledge at their own pace will help them much more than pushing them. We can only push ourselves to rise up to the challenge. If they're up to the challenge, they will push themselves. There is a fine line between the two. It's like helping a butterfly dry its wings as it emerges from the cocoon. If you think you can take a hair dryer and speed up the process, you will only stunt its growth. The colors and the wings won't fully open and develop, but will dry just where they are. The butterfly won't be able to fly with those stunted wings. It must take the time it needs to develop all the colors and patterns before drying its wings.

In nature, things must take their course and not be rushed. So keep your mind open to accept knowledge and grow but don't feel the necessity to rush the process, stunting your own growth or that of others.

EXERCISE

When you write down answers to the following questions, you'll find that this helps you to register and define these concepts more solidly as your hands send signals to your brain.

1. Do you feel that learning is the key to growth?
2. Are you open to learning new things, or do you feel you know enough?
3. Do you approach new knowledge with an excitement because it helps you grow, or do you see it merely as something boring that needs to be done to pass exams?
4. Do you listen to others with an open mind and then choose to agree or disagree, or do you simply shut people out because they think differently than you?

REMINDER

- Learning is growth. Listen more. Read more. A person who doesn't read is no better than one who can't read. If you don't use your skills, you lose them.
- By all means, be selective about what you read or listen to, as you're absorbing—consciously or unconsciously—what is around you.

Notes

Notes

Gratitude and Mindfulness

By consciously choosing each bite that you take, you are welcoming that particular food into your body. It then becomes your sustenance, serving your health and all your capacities. As you enter into the Spiritual Zone, you will learn that, in awakened consciousness, every action, no matter how small, will intentionally support your end result.

—Gary Quinn, *Living in the Spiritual Zone*

Father, bless this food, and bless all who have contributed to bringing it to my table. Bless all who share my table. Let this food nourish my body and bring health and vitality to every cell, every pore, every organ and every system in my body.

—My prayer before meals

When I pray, I occasionally get into a zone and express my gratitude in my own words that are simple but that I connect with, words that are meaningful for me, that evoke certain memories and emotions in me. The prayer above came to me a few days after the following incident jolted my awareness.

There was a time when I would read the "Dear Abby" advice column in the *Los Angeles Times* quite religiously. The questions or stories from people always fascinated me, and I learned a lot from these glimpses into the minds of people I would never meet but whom I felt I came to know through this column. One day, there was a story from a man whose colleague, during a discussion at work expressed that, as the man of the house, he was the one who worked hard to put food on the table, so he felt that his children should thank him for providing the meals instead of some unknown or unseen God. When he got home, he shared his colleague's story with his wife and joked about it, saying that maybe their children should thank him for the food that he provides.

As they sat down to dinner that night and said grace, his young son, who had heard the father's comment, looked at his father and said, "Thank you, Father, for the food," and then he closed his eyes and said, "Thank you, God, for my father."

This story touched me and got me thinking about how many people contribute to every meal that we put on the table. For example, when you have scrambled eggs and toast with coffee for breakfast, think of where each ingredient originated and how it was brought together to make the meal you're now about to consume.

Let us start with the egg to comprehend the immensity of the chain.

The farmer raised the hen. The hen was hatched from an egg, and the hen laid eggs that the farmer sold or hatched, and so on, going back infinitely.

The farmer was raised by his parents and their parents before that and so on, going back infinitely. The same is true of

- the person who prepared and sold the feed;
- the ingredients that this person used to prepare the feed came from many different sources;
- the hen that laid the eggs;
- and the people who cleaned, packaged, and shipped the eggs;
- and the shipping company that transported the eggs;
- and the market that sold the eggs;
- and the person who purchased the eggs;
- and the person who cooked the eggs using butter, salt, and pepper;

- and where the butter and salt and pepper came from;
- and on and on.

I think you get the picture.

Yet, how often do we mindlessly throw away the food and disrespect the efforts of those who have worked in this chain to create this nourishing meal. Not only food, but also we even consider people dispensable and dispose of them without a second thought. We forget how connected and interdependent we all are. We aren't isolated beings existing as individuals only, but we're connected like the drops of water that make up the ocean.

When we start seeing the underlying connections, we'll realize that nothing great was ever achieved by one individual alone. Similarly, all the cells connect to form our bodies. Each individual is like a cell in the "body" of the universe. If we but sit and think for a few moments each day to recognize the enormity of our connection, we'll perceive unity in diversity.

Our thoughts are powerful tools. We don't have to understand how electricity or radio waves work, but we accept that they do exist and work, yet we sell ourselves short and fail to realize the enormous power of our own being. We're awed by the technology and gadgets that man creates, but we fail to perceive and comprehend the enigmatic Being that created man, who creates the gadgets we so admire.

EXERCISE

1. Write down every day (preferably, or at least whenever you can) five things that you're grateful for—these can be big events like you winning a competition or small, everyday things like someone smiling at you.
2. Use natural resources mindfully. Before tossing out something, think if you can reuse it.
3. At social functions or buffets, where food is offered, take only small quantities that you know you can finish. If you want more, you can always go back for more.

4. Meditate on your connection to the world around you. Remember you breathe the oxygen that the trees give out.
5. Spend some time in nature regularly.
6. Write down the ways you can make a difference by changing your consuming habits.

REMINDER

- Your thoughts and actions make a difference, no matter how big or small.
- The longest journey begins with one step. Even the smallest change for the better has an impact.

Notes

Notes

Understanding the Healing Powers of Death

in Simple Terms

> To the well-organized mind, death is but the next great adventure.
>
> —J. K. Rowling

B ased on my study of religious teaching, I believe the first thing to understand is that our bodies are like vehicles that allow us to navigate through life. We are not our bodies. Just as we have cars or other vehicles to take us to different places, operated by a driver, the driver isn't the vehicle. He operates the vehicle. Similarly, the soul, as the driver, uses the body as the vehicle to help us experience life and learn lessons. It's imperative that we take care of our bodies to keep them in working order, just as we would make sure that our cars are in good working condition to get us to and from work and other destinations.

Occasionally, even new cars can have defects, so manufacturers have to recall them. Sometimes, being careless with maintenance or driving, we can cause accidents that render cars temporarily inoperable, so we have to wait until they are repaired. At other times, accidents can total cars beyond repair, so we end up having to replace them.

Similarly, our bodies can become inoperable if we don't take proper care or if we expose them to unhealthy conditions, or simply not allow time to recover by constantly pushing them beyond reasonable working capacities.

Older cars start to break down more frequently, so we replace those with new or slightly used cars because we still need to do a lot more driving than the older car is capable of. Like the older cars, our bodies start to slow down, but our souls aren't done learning all the lessons that they need to learn. When our bodies finally give out, our souls go back home to prepare for the next round. If we learned all the lessons that we came to learn previously, we move on to the next set of experiences, just as one would move up to the next grade in school. If we didn't complete our lessons, then we simply had to repeat the experiences and stay in the same grade for another year.

Another analogy that can help one understand this process is a stage play. There are a few acts in a play, and the characters appear and disappear as they've conveyed their messages or said their lines. Some characters are in every scene, but others are only there for very brief periods. We don't know when someone will show up or when it will be his or her last appearance. In life, the characters appear as they're meant to share their stories or convey their messages, or simply stay and see the whole project to its logical end.

Life is an endless journey in which people come and go, say their lines, convey their messages, learn their lessons, celebrate their wins, and bemoan their losses. Just as at the end of the school day it feels good to go home, rest, and relax before doing your homework and preparing for the next day of school, at the end of our lives, it is a blessing that we get to go home, be critiqued by our guides, and figure out where we excelled or where we failed. Then, after a period of rest, we prepare for our next lives. Our guides, masters, and teachers help us choose what lessons we still need to learn and what conditions we'll need to help us achieve those goals, what will make us challenge ourselves, or to choose a simpler curriculum for an easier life. Although we all eventually have to learn the lessons we need to, we have a choice of how quickly or how slowly we do that.

For our journeys, we (the Spirit) are equipped with souls that keep us connected to our authentic selves, egos that help us navigate ourselves in this world and help us define where our separation lines are, and bodies to function as our vehicles. The ego is like the CEO of a corporation. It has great power and authority, but it must always remember that it isn't the owner of the company. It's just someone who has been appointed to run it on behalf of the owner. If it forgets and gets drunk on its own power or sense of self, it starts making bad judgments and poor decisions. If it oversteps the boundaries, blinded by its own sense of self-importance, it starts to operate as a poor master. It's a great servant, performing very important and useful tasks, shielding us from harm and protecting us from getting lost in this vast jungle. If we lose our egos, then we give too much, even at the cost of ourselves. Hence, it's important to find a balance between self-preservation and helping others. We need a sense of self and self-worth and a healthy dose of committing to completing the tasks we've taken on. While it's noble to help others if they need help, we need to remind ourselves that we can't and shouldn't live life for them. If we lose our own identity, we'll overcompensate by doing too much for others, thus trying to control them because we've lost control of our own actions.

Ironically, we often take better care of our possessions that we have "paid for" in hard-earned money than we do of what we've been "given." Often, we even see it as a liability. We abuse it, misuse it, and mindlessly endanger it. When life gets tough or throws us a curve ball, we claim that we didn't ask to be born, and sometimes even try to end our own lives. Many of us have been at that point sometime in our lives. Some have gotten past it, others have taken action, and some unfortunately have even done so successfully, leaving loved ones with so many unanswered questions. Some people just pack in every hurt, every negative emotion, and every pain until they feel so overwhelmed by it all and feel that they can't take any more of it, so they check out.

On the other hand, some keep giving and giving until they feel so empty that nothing matters, and they have nothing left to give or nothing more to live for. So they check out! In the first case, they forget to release enough negativity to create space for positivity so they can find a balance. In the second scenario, they keep giving up everything they have to others, but think it selfish to replenish their own reserves. If you plan a trip to the Bahamas, book your tickets, and embark on your journey, but instead of going all the way to the Bahamas, you suddenly turn around after flying to Florida and refuse to get on to the ship, your friends and family will have endless questions. In this scenario, you'll be around to answer the questions. When you commit suicide midlife, you're no longer around to do so, leaving near and dear ones wondering where they failed or what they could have done differently. They would even experience guilt for not being more aware and failing to recognize the signs. The reality is that they have been so busy dealing with their own reality that they failed to recognize your troubles.

While untimely and unexpected death of a loved one can be devastating, leaving behind more questions than answers, death at the end of a life lived fully and well can be celebrated as a well-earned ticket home. Family and friends who understand the process of life celebrate with the departed soul, wish it well on its journey forward, even though they know they will miss this person's presence. They will cherish the memories of time spent together, grieve the loss, but in time, resume their own journeys here on this earth. When a soul truly understands the healing power of death, it no longer holds on to life in fear of the unknown. Yes, you will have to meet your Maker, your guides, and teachers to assess how and where you succeeded or failed in fulfilling your life's mission. You will have to pay your karmic debts by seeing how your actions hurt or helped others. Seeing the results of those and feeling the devastation others felt because of your actions will help you understand where you could have made better choices.

Most of us are so afraid to face ourselves and what we imagine is waiting for us based on our limited understanding of the purposes of our lives and journeys of our souls that we fight the transition, choosing to suffer illness and pain instead of seeking relief from them. A greater understanding can help free us and allow the healing to take place.

EXERCISE

By answering the following questions, you will be able to gain insight into your own actions.

1. How do you react when you hear of the death of a loved one?
2. What does death mean to you?
3. Do you think that the ending of a relationship, job, friendship, or even the loss of a limb is like death on a smaller scale?
4. How do you grieve a loss?
5. Do you allow time to grieve, or do you think that is a sign of weakness, so you put on a brave front and carry on?
6. Do you totally succumb to the loss and think your life is over, or do you feel that you can get up, pick up the pieces, and pull yourself together to move forward?

REMINDER

- There are new beginnings everywhere, no matter how great the loss. Nature loses everything in fall and hibernates in winter but brings back everything to life in spring to flourish in summer.
- Losses are uncompromising teachers that either break us or make us stronger, depending on how we choose to learn from them.

Notes

Notes

Choices

Life presents many choices. The choices we make determine our future.

—Catherine Pulsifer

Life is a series of small choices. The choice we make in the moment will determine where we end up and what becomes available to us to choose from next, depending on what we chose at each junction. We can go left, right, forward, backward, or stay where we are. This thread will eventually take us to a place where we planned to be or simply where we drifted because we didn't pay attention to the small daily choices that we made. When we choose one direction, we're in a new place, and that presents us with a new set of choices again.

Each choice is valid, but varies with your goal. If you're clear about your destination, you can choose easily. If you're not, then you're confused and have to deliberate longer.

You learn from everything. Even when you get lost, you can learn by looking back and seeing where you took the detour or missed the detour that you should have taken so that it took you in a different direction from where you wanted to go.

If you're traveling long distance to faraway places, you can take the freeways/highways that will take you to your destination faster, but you will miss the sights on the way. If you have enough time, you can take local streets, go through towns and villages, meet people, stop and rest, and still get there.

Similarly, in life, learn to enjoy the journey instead of always rushing to the destination. Find a balance that's right for you. There are many valid paths. Your journey will depend on your goals, destination, resources, time available, and choices.

The great thing about this process is that if we catch ourselves early by staying in touch with our authentic selves, we won't drift too far from where we were headed. So, it's advisable to periodically, pause, assess, and determine if we're on track. If we've strayed off course a bit, we aren't too far off to back track easily.

On the other hand, if we don't take the time to check in with ourselves at reasonable intervals, when we do stop to check, because the landscape is no longer familiar or what we'd thought it should be at this stage, we may find ourselves in a totally different environment. The upside on that is that life is a process. As we journey on, we aren't bound to stay lost but can find our way back. It may take longer to resume the journey, or it may be an uphill battle now, but it can be done. We can either backtrack or find other roads that will take us and connect to the road we'd decided to take originally. It will take a little longer, but we'll gain experience as we enjoy new vistas.

The importance of making the right choices is very aptly stated in the fable of the two wolves, where the grandfather tells his son that there are two wolves inside each of us. The wolves refer to the good and evil that we're all capable of. However, the wolf that wins is the one that we feed the most.

Nothing is ever hopeless. We just need to revisit our perspectives and realign our goals instead of beating ourselves up for veering off course. Know that, sometimes, the universe purposely lets us lose our way in order for us to find new destinations that we may not have otherwise explored because it knows that we'll benefit from the experience. As we travel along this road, we'll find that these new experiences will better prepare us to deal with what the purpose of our lives is and the destination we're headed to.

Nothing in life is ever lost. It just meets us dressed in a different garb, so, journey on. May your journey be peaceful, educational, exciting, and fruitful.

Just as you exercise for physical fitness, similarly, there are practices for mental, emotional, and spiritual health.

- Should we go or stay?
- Will we choose the high road or the low road?
- Is it better to choose the well-trodden path or the road less traveled?

Use caution. Some adventurous spirits throw caution to the wind. Their journeys may be turbulent and painful, but they can still learn from them. Sometimes one can be cautious but still have moments of adventurous breakthroughs.

My reality is shaped by

- what I see around me;
- what I watch on screens;
- what I read in books, magazines, newspapers;
- what I think in my mind; and
- what I feel in my heart.

My realty is expressed by

- what I speak;
- how I speak; and
- what I write.

My reality is known by

- if I keep good company or bad company;
- if I pull up others to lift and elevate them or put others down to crush and suppress them;
- if I am kind or cruel to others; and
- the choices I make every day.

EXERCISE

Observe your behavior for a week and write down how you make choices. Especially note whether you make conscious decisions for small choices also or only ponder on major life choices.

1. Do you behave impulsively all the time or occasionally?
2. Do you often make choices that you regret later?
3. Write down all the choices you made—small and big—for one day (e.g., about what food to eat, eating less or more, work/homework, traffic, getting angry or staying calm, watching TV, how long, procrastinating, chores, friends, and so on).
4. Write down the good or bad consequences of your choices from the previous day.
5. Are you happy with the choices you made?
6. If you had given a little more thought, what would you have chosen differently?

REMINDER

- With a little patience and practice, you can learn to think before choosing certain actions rather than regret your choices later.
- Your ability to manage your choices will give you more control over the consequences.
- Popular choices aren't always the right choices, so choose wisely in the moment rather than impulsively.
- Don't beat yourself up if you make the wrong choices, but forgive yourself and learn from it. Forgiving yourself for a wrong choice isn't the same as making excuses. You learn nothing from making excuses.

Notes

Notes

Communicating Efficiently, Especially between Parents and Teenagers

> The most important thing in communication is hearing what isn't being said. The art of reading between the lines is a lifelong quest of the wise.
>
> —Shannon L. Alder

Learning to communicate with people around you is an absolute must. It's important to voice your feelings, thoughts, and ideas, and thus validate your existence. It's imperative to recognize that you're important, you're worthy of being here, and what you have to share is valuable.

As we transition from childhood to the teenage years, hormones kick in, our bodies go through numerous changes, and we seem to no longer recognize ourselves. Many of us feel that we're the only ones going through these processes, and we might hide, further isolating ourselves and adding to our loneliness.

While it is true that one can only know of one's own feelings and thoughts, we can certainly learn from others by sharing these. We think no one loves this dark entity that's now consumed with sexual thoughts due to the hormonal changes, and we're embarrassed about it—we think that our bodies are no longer cute but awkward. We start to think there is something wrong with us and so we're unsure of ourselves. Everyone else seems so sure of themselves and seems to be blossoming. But that's only because on the inside they are feeling as vulnerable as you, so they show up with this facade to fool everyone. It's often the person who seems to laugh the most or appears the most confident who gets so good at hiding behind a strong front that he or she never lets you in to see his or her insecurities and weaknesses.

This is why now communication is more important than ever. Just knowing and recognizing that almost everyone is feeling the same and that this is a normal part of the transition is helpful.

For parents, this is a difficult period, because the sweet child who adored the parents and thought they were the best people in the world are now "controlling" and so "overbearing," always telling the child what to do. For the children who are now ready to spread their wings but who still want to be sheltered, it's a period of confusing emotions.

The first time I spoke back defiantly to my father, when he wouldn't let me attend an event with my friends without adult supervision, he sat me down and talked to me. He explained that while he understood that I wanted to be more independent, this was the age where teenagers want the "privileges of a child" without taking "responsibilities of an adult." I would need to make a choice and decide which one I wanted. I couldn't have both. Did I still want to enjoy the benefits of being taken care of by my parents while I abide by their rules and respect their decisions, or did I take responsibility as an adult and take care of myself so I could live as I chose to.

This is also when parents need to be very firm with differentiating between *privacy* and *secrecy.* Respect your child's privacy but don't encourage secrecy in the guise of privacy. Don't isolate the child even more. There is a very fine line there. Encourage children to share their secret fears and insecurities. Don't make fun of them or their confidences. At this age, they're very volatile and vulnerable, so don't break their trust.

On the other hand, also remember that if you misunderstand or make a mistake, you must forgive yourself. Know that child rearing doesn't come with a manual. Each child's personality is different, even though there's a common thread to the entire transition process.

Look out for the classic signs of either extreme—either too withdrawn or too confident and too driven. There's a different kind of pressure that each child puts on his- or herself. If the child feels worthless, not needed, or not valued, he or she will withdraw and not care. On the other hand, with a stronger personality, the same feelings may translate into the child being driven to prove that he or she is perfect but never believing that he or she has quite mastered it. Thus, the child always strives for more or feels like a failure if he or she isn't the best at everything.

It's important at this age for a child to understand that failing at something or not succeeding at the first attempt doesn't mean the child is a failure. It's important for children to learn that if they fall, they only need to get up, dust themselves off, and try again. These values need to be stated and restated time and again. Children will only hear what they believe or what they want to hear. They'll only absorb what validates their belief or their opinion of themselves.

During her teens, my daughter got a wart on her lip. She was convinced that she was ugly and that no one loved her. She was ready to run away from home. The more I tried to explain to her how much I loved her, the more convinced she became that I was only saying it because I "had to" since I was her mother. Eventually, I told her that I could say it till I was blue in the face, but it wouldn't matter until she believed that she was lovable and that I did love her. That got her to think and wonder, although it took many more years before she actually believed it.

Another example that comes to mind is from the mother and daughter who were guests on *The Merv Griffin Show*, a talk show in the 1980s. The girl was gorgeous, but she had attempted suicide several times because she felt she was "the ugliest person on earth," so no one loved her. Her mother could not convince her otherwise, so she sought help. With counseling, the girl was able to let go of her false beliefs and recognize where those had originated. Now, she opted to appear on the talk show to let other teenagers know that they too could receive help and change the warped image of themselves.

Children need to understand that while anger, resentment, hatred, and dislike are valid emotions that need to be handled and expressed in an appropriate way, it's okay for them to express them.

CHILDREN

The transition from childhood to adulthood is a process. No one is perfect—not you, not your parents—and that's okay.

Your rights are my responsibilities just as my rights are your responsibilities. Don't be so busy demanding your rights that you forget your responsibilities.

Don't expect the world from your parents or yourself but expect the best you both are capable of. This is dynamic and should keep changing and getting better as each one grows and experiences life while learning from those experiences.

Spend some time in complete silence—of the mind and body—to develop a greater understanding of yourself, your parents, and the world.

Forgive yourself for what you think you failed at, and your parents and others for where you think they failed you or for what you think they didn't deliver—in order to move forward and break the generational negative cycles.

Make sure your expectations are realistic. By all means, dream of reaching for the moon and the stars, but also realize that you can't just be a pilot flying an airplane to do that literally, but you will need to become an astronaut and use a rocket—more effort, more expense, and more time. Are you willing to make that investment?

PARENTS

Give roots first for stability and then let your children grow wings to fly out. Let them grow like beautiful, sturdy trees with strong roots and trunks for support. Then nourish the branches as they grow out to reach for the sky.

Don't beat yourself up if you fall or fail. Remember that you're human and doing your own growing up also.

You're still the parent. You're still in charge. Your house, your rules. Remember: rivers are beautiful and very useful, but if they follow the path of least resistance, they become crooked, and if not contained properly, they will overflow and wreak havoc. Allow your children a reasonable amount of freedom to flow freely, but don't let them take over.

Teach them the right way to balance rights and responsibilities.

Have respect for yourself, your children, their teachers, and for learning.

Don't demand respect; command it. Know that they are learning *everything* from you. Don't ask them to "do as you say, not as you do." In your old age, your *children* won't feed you, but the *values* you have taught them will. Of course, there will always be some who won't incorporate those values, but for the most part, they'll come through.

Life isn't one big choice, but a series of small choices, and each one will determine where you finally end up.

An understanding of the world and your own parents is very important.

Forgive yourself for what you think you failed at, and forgive your parents and others for the areas in which you think they failed you or for what you think they didn't deliver, in order to move forward and break the generational negative cycles.

EXERCISE

Fill in the blanks:

1. Communication means _____
   _____.

2. When I share information with others, I feel _____
   _____.

3. A well-written article is also a _____
   _____.

Answer the following questions:

1. Do you merely talk, or do you communicate?
2. Is it possible to talk without communicating? If yes, what is the difference?

3. Have your family and friends told you they appreciate how you communicate with them, or do they complain that you don't communicate well?

4. When others talk to you, do you sometimes feel that their words are saying something different from what their demeanor or actions are indicating?

5. Can you communicate without talking?

REMINDER

- Understanding the difference between communication and merely talking can reduce misunderstandings and hurt feelings.
- Sometimes what you say is merely covering how you feel so there's no real communication.
- It's okay not to communicate with everyone, but it's very important to communicate well with those close to you.
- People who learn to communicate well through speech or their writings can become great orators or writers.

Notes

Notes

Giving Yourself Permission

This is your world. Shape it, or somebody else will.

—Unknown

I offer here a simplified way of working with your brain to take charge of your actions and habits to change your life. You might even consider it oversimplified. The only requirement is that you believe it to be true. If you bring in doubt and do this with the attitude that it won't happen, then that's what will transpire, since that's what your brain is hearing from you. However, since trying doesn't hurt you but may help you, it might be worth a shot.

Please note this isn't presented as a cure-all. Nothing is implied or stated that this replaces professional medical opinion. It doesn't make any promises of changing your lives. There are many factors that go into making change happen, and it will be a different combination for everyone. The only common factors that will mobilize this transformation is your presence, commitment, faith, belief, and persistence. It's definitely possible. So do what you can, wholeheartedly, and you'll surprise yourself.

- Use it for what surfaces during the day for that day, because your subconscious is trying to draw your attention to something by bringing to the surface whatever is holding you back or what the underlying negative pattern is.

- Use only positive affirmations, as your brain identifies better with that. For example, say you will do something rather than saying that you won't do it anymore.

- Use these whenever you find that as soon as you close your eyes to meditate, relax, or sleep, your brain seems to be taking over with negative thoughts rushing in because of the space created.

- Although you can say these at any time, I've found that it works best when I say it just before I go to sleep. It seems the subconscious mind is more receptive and isn't blocked by conscious mind telling it that it won't work.

- You see, our *conscious minds* are like the reception desk in a multistoried building that houses a variety of offices and businesses. If you rent space there and have security clearance, you can come and go as needed. There are different levels of clearance. Executives or business owners working in or renting space in the building have total clearance. Employees of the businesses have restricted access and are limited to office hours. Visitors and clients must check with the receptionist, sign in, state where they are going and who they are going to see. The receptionist then calls the person to verify, unless he or she has already been provided a list of people who have appointments that day. Once this is verified, the visitor or the client is given directions and allowed to go to the appointment.

Similarly, in our *conscious minds*, the brain receives the information coming through the eyes and ears, perceives the information, analyzes it, accepts or rejects it, and once accepted, lets it in. Our brains then begin to recognize the pattern, and after a while, this information becomes part of our *subconscious* brains, and we repeat it without even realizing sometimes that we're doing it. It's similar to doing a security check on a new employee and possibly having a probationary period, but once given clearance, the need to check access every time is eliminated. As our conscious brain accepts our actions and behaviors and considers those safe and productive, it gives permission to the *subconscious* brain to repeat it without constant supervision. For example, when we meet someone for the first time, we're cautious initially, but after some time, when we know that we can trust that person, we relax and welcome him into our fold.

Subconscious mind is the storage house. Once the information has been analyzed by the brain and accepted or rejected, then it's moved to the subconscious and stays there until it needs to be recalled or referenced. This is why we react to words or actions of others, often without knowing why because by now we're no longer consciously aware of how or why we came to those conclusions.

Computer memory is like our brain memory. We can open a few windows at a time, but if we open too many, the conscious memory isn't enough to handle all these windows, and the computer crashes. The information is there in the computer's memory, but can be recalled or worked with only in small segments.

In the same manner, there's so much knowledge, information, and inherent wisdom in our subconscious that we aren't even aware of.

This is why it is imperative that we periodically "clean house," to release information that is no longer serving us, which we may have picked up along the way. This also helps us to delve deeper and understand, if we allow ourselves to go back far enough, how children are born with unbelievable talents or other behavioral or physical traits.

When you learn a new technique, practice it till it becomes as natural as breathing—something that you do without any conscious effort but you feel its lack if it doesn't work. However, remember that this isn't the only technique that can help you. After some time, if you feel it no longer works, maybe that's because you have resolved the issue this was supposed to help with, and you're ready to learn something new. Blended foods that are necessary for a baby to be able to digest are needed less and less as his or her teeth start to come in and the baby gets more proficient at biting and chewing. The baby still has to wait some more to be able to eat hard foods until all the teeth are in and he or she is able to chew properly. So, also, you should allow enough time for a new technique to work before moving on to something else.

Before you sleep, sit for five minutes or more at the edge of your bed, on a chair, or on the floor, and say any of the following that resonate with you or that you connect with. Don't limit yourself to these only. Use your imagination, speak from the heart, and give yourself permission to voice what you want to. This is *your* brain you're talking to. You're the only one in charge here.

I give my brain permission to

- enjoy a restful and restorative sleep;
- be calm and collected;
- release excess weight;
- be organized;
- be happy;
- forgive myself and others (general) or _____ (specific);
- love myself;
- allow myself to be loved;
- believe I am worthy of love;
- know that I am worthy of love;
- open my heart;
- trust;
- focus;
- have faith; and
- replace negative thoughts with positive ones.
  You can add whatever else you want to change or reinforce to this list.

EXERCISE

To better understand yourself, look for answers to the following questions. A lot of information can be found in books or on the internet. By doing this yourself, instead of just being given the answers, you will have a clearer understanding:

1. What is the difference between the brain and the mind?
2. Why is my brain sometimes not able to recall the information when I need it?

3. Why does my mind wander when I'm trying to focus?
4. Why do I need to give my brain permission to change messages programmed in the subconscious mind?

REMINDER

- The brain is like the hardware in the computer, and the mind is like the software.
- By changing the messages sent to the brain, you can change the stories in the conscious and subconscious mind.
- By understanding how the brain and the mind function, you can take charge of your actions and, as a consequence, have better control over your behaviors.

Notes

Notes

Self-Reflection

If you don't love yourself, you'll always be chasing after people who don't love you either.

—Mandy Hale

Pay close attention to what you see, hear, and think, for that will tell you where you are in your journey. This is especially true if you feel a connection or feel your heart, mind, and soul responding in some way. It may be something you need to address and deal with or simply let go. It could be what is holding you down or back, or it could be telling you what direction you need to take. Sometimes it is simply a test to see how well you have learned what you needed to, by tempting you to revert to your old ways.

Correct interpretation is key, and for that, a clear and uncluttered mind is required. We live our lives on so many levels—in relationships with family and friends, in relationships with our significant others, in relationships with society, with our coworkers, and most important of all, in relationships with ourselves as human beings, with our own ethics and morality.

Often, there are conflicts in our decisions because what we feel is good for us may not work for our family or may not be conducive to the greater good of humankind. We have to learn to prioritize. While our main priority is to live lives that promote the growth of our souls, it's imperative to understand that what works for that growth may appear to be a selfish act. Understanding the difference between what *appears* to be selfish versus what *is* selfish will help with making a better choice.

Reflect on your thoughts and actions. Clean house frequently. Forgive yourself and others. Understand that forgiving doesn't mean justifying or validating mistakes, because no one is perfect. It simply means that upon reflection, you have realized that a decision or an action that you thought was right actually hurt a lot of people, and it wasn't right, even though in your limited understanding and belief at that time, you didn't perceive it as wrong. Atone for the same, resolve not to repeat it, and move on. Forgiving others means if someone reacted harshly to what your words or actions triggered in him or her or if someone was violent in thought, speech, or action toward you, from your new space of better understanding, forgive that person because you realize that that person is doing the best based on where he or she is in life. You're not responsible for another person's behavior or choices. Forgiving someone doesn't mean you weren't hurt; it means you no longer hold yourself in that negative space and wish to remove yourself and move on to something better.

Reflect on this thought. You're not your disease. You *may have* a "dis-ease" because of some upset in your body. It may even be deep set if you didn't catch it in time, but you *are not* the "dis-ease." Go deep inside your essence to understand who you truly are. When you do, it will become clear to you that you have immense power that you didn't recognize or use properly. This means that if you put your energies to heal yourself, you can. However, there are also many other factors that either prevent you from doing that or dilute your energies: negative emotions, years or sometimes lifetimes of conditioning, beliefs that keep you locked in a certain mindset so you expect only those results. But that is okay, as it is part of the learning process. When you learn to release the debris that has buried your potential and diverted your focus to keep you from developing that potential, you can slowly make your way back to the source of your power and claim it.

EXERCISE

Ask yourself the following questions:

1. Do you take the time to reflect on your thoughts and actions?
2. Are you constantly going from one activity to another without giving much thought to why you do that?
3. Do you feel like life is a roller coaster?
4. Do you think that if you take the time for reflection you're wasting time?

REMINDER

- Taking the time to reflect is like maintenance for machines. It's important to keep them clean, well oiled, and in good working order to ensure fewer breakdowns.
- By reflecting on your actions, you can determine whether what you're doing is still relevant and productive instead of continuing to do what worked before but isn't necessary now. You can also see if there are better and different ways to do what you need to do.
- By periodically examining your activity, you can save time in the long run by eliminating superfluous things and replacing old methods with newer, more efficient ones.

Notes

Notes

Nature of Healing

Be brave enough to heal yourself even when it hurts.
—Bianca Sparacino, *The Strength in Our Scars*

The soul always knows what to do to heal itself. The challenge is to silence the mind.

—Caroline Myss

When the wound is deep, dressed, and medicated, you don't feel as much pain as you do when it starts to heal, is now closer to the surface of the skin, is less medicated, and isn't bandaged to allow the scab to form. This is the next stage in healing a wound, but it is very painful.

The steps described above in the healing of a physical wound are similar to the ones in the healing of mental, psychological, and emotional wounds.

When you become aware of the painful memories, know that what you had "forgotten" and buried deep in the recesses of your subconscious is now getting ready to be released so that it won't trigger unpleasant reactions anymore. You're now getting ready to take charge of your responses and take responsibility for your actions.

However, this is also the stage of healing that takes the longest. There's resistance from the mind that wants to hold on to its stories, rather than let the brain be in charge again. It has grown comfortable in its niche of being the "injured" one receiving the attention and care. If that's gone, what will it do with itself?

There's resistance because it would imply that what you have believed up till now isn't correct. There's anger at facing your helplessness and inability to have done anything about what happened to cause that hurt, whether as a child or as an adult. There's grief at the loss of your beliefs and your truth as you have lived with it. There's disillusionment at the realization that there are two sides to every story and one side isn't always right or the other side always wrong. Things are seldom black and white. There's a lot of overlapping, causing there to be a large area of various shades of gray.

There is fear of moving forward into unknown territory. You have become familiar with what you have lived with. What if the new beliefs and truths hurt even more? And finally, there is the resistance and refusal to forgive. Somehow, forgiveness will make you feel weak or imply that you weren't wronged. It would also mean that justice wouldn't have been served. The wrongs that you experienced won't have been avenged.

But this is still an illusion. The truth is that you will still be carrying the burden that you're trying to release, and it will still be the one in control, not you.

The best way to get rid of the darkness is to light a candle or flip the switch on. Someone said that there isn't enough darkness in the world to put out the light of one candle. Flipping the switch on will shine the light *only* if there is an electric connection, and how much light it actually shines will depend on how powerful the connection is and how clear and what strength the bulb is. If there is a surge of power but the bulb is weak, it will explode.

Take your time. Be cautious but let go of fear. Strengthen your spiritual connection with the universe or higher power (like the unseen electric connection that powers the bulb) with mindfulness, meditation, and heartfelt prayer. Replace doubt, fear, and anger with trust, love, and forgiveness slowly and cautiously.

Here is an experiment for you to try. Take two cups. Fill one with mud, and let the mud dry and become caked to the cup. When that is done, put sand in the other cup. Then place those under two faucets with running water. Let the water run until it runs clear and all the mud and sand are washed out. You will notice that the caked mud takes a lot longer to clear out than the sand. Sand is loose, so it washes out faster. The dried and caked mud has to first moisten and soften before the water can wash it out. How long it takes to replace negative thoughts and beliefs with positive ones to "clean house" will depend on how long they have been a part of you and how tightly you hold on to them.

Forgive yourself. Be patient with yourself. You will then be able to have patience with and extend forgiveness to others. Remember improvement begins with "I."

EXERCISE

Ask yourself the following questions:

1. What did you learn from the mud versus sand experiment?
2. What is the difference between the mind and the brain?
3. Why is forgiveness so important?
4. How can forgiving the person who hurt you allow you to move on?

REMINDER

- The mind keeps us lost in stories. The brain tells us how it is.
- Forgiving helps us get rid of the toxic, negative thoughts. This way we no longer keep drinking the poison while hoping the other person will die.
- Understand that while the healing process is often painful, the "infection" must be treated for total healing to take place.

Notes

Notes

Fables and Stories

Fables have been told over generations in simple formats to help children understand the consequences of their actions or inactions and pay attention to their thoughts and their words.

I heard most of these fables from my parents and grandparents or read them in school courses.

The stories I share here are personal experiences that are closest to my heart and that have shaped my thinking, actions, and behavior so that these can guide and help others also to be hopeful in situations where they may feel hopeless or encourage them to reach out for help.

Some of the fables shared here have been retold in my own words as I best remember them. Thus, it is an acknowledgment of how deeply their messages stated in simple terms have stayed with me over the decades, which I now share with a whole new audience.

Faith

> For what I have received may the Lord make me truly
> thankful. And more truly for what I have not received.
>
> —Storm Jameson

The master sat pondering on how to resolve his disciple's dilemma. The disciple had asked why things were always going wrong for him. It seemed that, no matter how hard he tried, he could not catch a break. Whatever he wanted or asked God for, he didn't get.

The master asked, "Do you pray?"

The disciple said, "I used to pray, but I don't pray anymore."

"Why?" the master asked.

"Well," the disciple said, "because I am mad at God. He is like our Father. When a child asks for something and his father refuses to give it to him, the child gets mad at his father and doesn't talk to him. I asked God for something, and He didn't give it to me, so I'm not talking to Him."

"You shouldn't get mad at God," the master said.

Before the Master could elaborate, the disciple's toddler son came into the room to play with his father. When he saw the sliced fruit on the table, he ran to the table to get some. As he got there, he saw a shiny knife and picked it up to play with it. The disciple took it from him, and the baby started crying.

"Why did you take the knife from the child?" the master asked. "Now you've made him cry. Give it back to him."

The disciple was astonished. "But if I give it to him, he'll cut himself!"

"But he is crying. He wants to play with it."

"Oh, don't worry," the disciple said. "He'll be distracted soon enough and will stop crying."

The master said, "Well, you've answered your own question. I was wondering how to explain it to you. You see, even as an earthly father, you know that what the child is asking for isn't good for him and could hurt him, so in your wisdom, you took it away even though it made him cry. You don't want him to cry, but you know that if you give him what he wants, it will be worse for him. You also know that he'll soon be distracted and forget about the knife.

"Heavenly Father is so much wiser than you. He knows that what you asked for isn't good for you, so he doesn't give it to you. You'll be upset for some time, but then you'll find something better.

"So, know that even when the answer to your prayer is no, it's an answer of love and not abandonment or punishment. Trust Him and have faith that there's a reason you didn't get what you asked for, because something better will come your way unless you block it with your fear of loss and lack of faith."[1]

MORAL

Have faith in the wisdom of a higher power and know that when no is the answer to your prayers, it is because something better is coming to you.

---

[1] Note: This story is based on an actual conversation that took place between my father and a religious leader.

The Cow and the Pig—
A Tale from India

The cow and the pig lived on the farm. The pig noticed that the farmer took great care of the cow, kept its stall clean, and washed it often. He let the cow out in the pasture to graze. He was very gentle and almost affectionate toward the cow.

However, the farmer's behavior toward the pig was different. While the farmer didn't treat the pig poorly, he also didn't take as good care of him. Oh yes, he was fed well, but this was to fatten him up so he would fetch a good price when he was sold to the butcher.

The pig wondered about that. All that the cow did was give milk. The pig gave his entire body. Every part of his body was used—the meat, bones, hooves, fat, skin. Nothing was wasted. Why then was the cow almost worshipped while the pig was shunned?

One day, the pig asked the cow, "Why is it that you're so respected when all you give is milk, and why am I shunned when I give my whole body?"

The cow replied, "It is so because I give of myself while I'm still alive."

In life, when people share their bounty with the less fortunate, they're honored and respected, while others, who may leave all their wealth and worldly goods to their families, are often resented. They only leave behind what no one can take with him or her upon death. After death, it doesn't make much difference to someone who may have had need of it before. Their relatives who are left behind may fight, or even kill in greed, for what they think they are entitled to.

MORAL

Helping others at the cost of your own needs adds more value to your gift.

Karma and Forgiveness

The man who has won millions at the cost of his conscience is a failure.

—B. C. Forbes

To forgive is to set a prisoner free and discover that the prisoner was you.

—Lewis B. Smedes,
ethicist and theologian

They will come back, come back again,
As long as the red earth rolls.
He never wasted a leaf or a tree,
Do you think He would squander souls?

—Rudyard Kipling,
"The Sack of the Gods"

I hold that when a person dies
His soul returns again to earth;
Arrayed in some new flesh-disguise
Another mother gives him birth.
With sturdier limbs and brighter brain
The old soul takes the road again.

—John Masefield, "A Creed"

Major Mohan Kumar knew he wasn't going to make it. The battle had been going on for a while, and he'd been hit by an enemy bullet. He pulled himself painfully to the side so he wouldn't be laying in the middle of the field, where he might accidentally trip someone. He looked around to see if his friend Captain Jai Sinha was around. Mohan needed to tell Jai something, and he didn't have much time left.

There was a momentary pause in the firing from the enemy lines. Captain Jai Sinha had seen his friend get hit, but he didn't know how bad it was. Now, since Jai had a few moments, he turned back to look for Mohan and saw him lying by the bushes, not moving. Jai quickly went over to see if any help was forthcoming and to assess the damage. He saw the gaping wound bleeding profusely. Jai tore Mohan's shirt and pressed the fabric into the wound to slow the bleeding. He held Mohan's hand and asked what he could do while they waited for the medic. Mohan could barely whisper. He looked at Jai and motioned for him to come closer. He then told Jai that he knew he wouldn't make it but wanted to make sure that a message was conveyed to his wife, Nisha. He wanted Jai to promise that he would deliver a message from him to Nisha that told her where she could find the money that Mohan had saved and hidden in case of such an event. She could get the money and start a small business to be able to support herself and their two children, since the pension wouldn't be enough to cover the ever-increasing expenses of the children's education and other expenses. Jai held his friend's hand and promised to do so. He comforted him as he saw him take his last breath.

A few months had passed since Jai's friend had died. He was now on his way home. He was devastated from losing his friend and was anxious to get home to his own family. He'd been married only a few months before he was deployed to the war zone.

As the train neared its destination, he started thinking. He wasn't going back to the army. He was sick of all the violence and dealing with trauma day in and day out. But he needed the money since he had not saved up for anything. Then he thought of Mohan and how wise he had been to think of his future. Jai felt his stomach turn at the thought of being the bearer of bad news to Mohan's wife, while he also felt happy to be giving her the good news about the money so she could move on with her life.

As he thought more and more about it, he realized that Nisha didn't know about the money. She had already been informed about her husband's death, so she must have moved on and made some decisions. It had been almost three months since Mohan died. He felt a stirring of greed and thought that if he got the money and kept it for himself, Nisha would never know. He and Kamini could start a business, and as they became more successful and made more money, he could then pay back Nisha. The more he thought about it, the more sense it made to him.

So, when he got home, after resting for a day or so, he headed to the hiding place that Mohan had told him about. It was an obscure place in the forest behind his house. It wasn't difficult to identify the tree near the stream, under which it was buried. He went there on the pretext of fishing, dug up the spot, and found the money in the can, exactly as Mohan had described to him. For a moment, Jai felt a twinge of guilt, but he quelled it by telling himself that he was just borrowing the money and that he intended to pay Nisha back when his business took off.

Jai saw that there was enough money to make a deposit on a gas station with a convenience store. He found a store for sale in a great location. Kamini helped him run the store, and they both worked hard to take it to the next level.

They were now running a profitable store, so they decided to expand their business and purchase another store. He remembered that he had to pay back Nisha the money that he had "borrowed." Then he told himself that if he used the savings to purchase another store instead, he could then pay it back with interest. She didn't need the money right away. Besides, she didn't even know about it.

Jai and Kamini were happy and prosperous. Now all they needed to complete their life was to have children. They had been trying for a while, but because of the stress of work and the long hours, Kamini had miscarried twice. Now they could afford to hire more help so Kamini could stay at home. But their dreams remained unfulfilled. They visited holy men and performed special rituals as advised. Finally, after almost a year and a half, they were blessed with a son.

They were happy to welcome the son, but their joy was tinged with sorrow because the son was born with a heart condition, and the doctors said that he may not live too long. They took him to the best doctors and got him the best treatments. Although their son, Sohan, survived, he remained sickly and needed constant care and various surgeries. Jai and Kamini loved their son and did all they could do to make him comfortable and feel better. Sadly, Sohan struggled with his health for seventeen years, and then finally, his heart gave out, and he died.

Jai and Kamini were devastated. They sought answers from holy men, asking why this had happened to them. Why had God punished them so?

The wise holy man told them that it wasn't God who had punished them; their own actions had brought this fate on them. Sohan was none other than the soul of Jai's friend, Mohan, who had come to collect the money that Jai had taken from him. The money Jai had spent on Sohan's treatment was equal to what he had taken from him. It took seventeen years to do that.

Jai was very angry and vowed revenge. The holy man shook his head and said that that was how karma worked and kept one constantly in a cycle of victim and perpetrator.

"You took Mohan's money, and he came back as your son to get it back from you. Now you're angry and want revenge, so you will come back in his life to get it from him. This is why forgiveness is so important. You see, if Mohan had forgiven you for your greed, he wouldn't have had to suffer the pain of ill health for years to get his money back. You would still have had to pay, maybe as a donation or to help someone else, to atone for the deceit, thus paying it forward. This would have taken care of your karma but wouldn't have angered you enough to want revenge, thus breaking the cycle."

QUESTIONS FOR DISCUSSION AND RESEARCH

1. What do you think of the story?
2. Do you believe in reincarnation? Would you like to learn more about it?

3. Do you believe in karma? How do you think it works?
4. Do you think that, in this story, karmic justice was served?
5. If you're refusing to forgive someone, ask yourself what is it that you're not forgiving yourself for in your interactions with that person.

NOTE

Since I grew up with a belief in reincarnation, it wasn't difficult for me explore the subject further. Those who are new to the concept may have questions that I can't guess at with my background. So, I've listed a few titles in the Suggested Reading section at the end of the book for you to begin. While there are numerous books on the subject and a ton of information on the internet, these are some of the books that offer multifaceted information for someone looking to know that reincarnation isn't just a belief of limited scope. As the readers start exploring, they will find that more and more relevant information will come their way. It's always prudent to be a little skeptical and to question some beliefs. However, it's wise to do so with an open mind and as a seeker of truth to get the answers. If you only do so with a closed mind and only with the intention to disprove it, you will be no further in your exploration than where you were to begin with.

For those who believe, no proof is necessary. For those who do not, no proof is enough.

You will also find interesting information on Bridey Murphy, Joan Grant, and Jenny Cockell, to name a few, who remembered some of their past lives.

MORAL

Our actions have long-term consequences that we sometimes don't see because of our shortsightedness.

Compliments to the Chef

Knowing you are a child of the creator of the universe changes everything.

—Rick Warren

Don't doubt the Creator because it is inconceivable that accidents alone could be the controller of this universe.

—Isaac Newton

Two friends were having a heated discussion about God. One of them was an atheist and didn't believe in any kind of God. The other one believed that since neither one of them or anybody else that they knew had created the beautiful world of nature, earth, planets, stars, and so on, there had to be some force that had created it all. It wasn't so significant what we called this force, but we simply could not deny it. Whether you believed in the theory of evolution or wanted scientific proof, this much was undisputed—that the Creator was magnificently represented by its creation.

Passionate and heated discussions followed, but they could not come to an agreement. They were now getting hungry and decided to set aside their discussion for another day to go enjoy a hearty meal at their favorite restaurant. They placed their orders and waited to get their food. When the waiter finally brought it, they both looked at the beautifully presented meal and savored its appetizing aroma. They started to eat and were absolutely thrilled with this treat for their taste buds that the aroma had promised. When the waiter came by to see how they were enjoying the meal and ask if they needed anything else, the atheist told him to convey his compliments to the chef. As he did so, his friend spoke up and asked, "Since there is no chef, who are you sending the compliments to?"

The atheist looked at his friend in confusion and asked, "Who do you think prepared this meal?"

The friend answered, "You did not see anyone prepare that meal, so how can you say that someone did?"

The atheist was getting annoyed with his friend's unreasonable argument. Of course someone had to have prepared the meal and just because he was in the kitchen and they could not see him didn't mean that there was no chef.

The friend then smiled and said, "You don't see the person who prepared the meal, but you *know* that because a meal has been prepared, there is a chef responsible for that. Yet you see a wonderful creation all around you that you know isn't created by you or me or anyone we know, but you find it difficult to believe that there is a Creator responsible for doing that? It isn't so important what you call Him, but you can't deny His existence."

MORAL

For those who believe, no proof is necessary. For those who do not, no proof is enough. Sometimes we just have to have faith.

Taking a Break

Rest when you're weary. Refresh and renew yourself,
your body, your mind, your spirit. Then get back to work.
— Ralph Marston

Rest and rejuvenate. Understand the importance of making deposits—you can't make withdrawals from your bank account if you have not made deposits. We know, understand and accept that about our bank accounts, but we ignore or forget about it regarding our "physical accounts." We either forget to eat or choose not to eat, or we eat the wrong kinds of food (like depositing fake currency) and expect to withdraw against it. We even deny ourselves rest because we feel that we have to constantly be productive.

The following story brings home the point in a very simple way.

Two lumberjacks decided to compete against each other to see who could chop more wood in a day.

One of them chopped wood for fifty minutes and then rested for ten minutes every hour. The other one kept chopping wood without stopping. At the end of the day, the one who took breaks had chopped more wood than his competitor had.

His competitor was very confused. He asked, "How were you able to chop more wood when you stopped for ten minutes every hour, but I chopped nonstop?"

The winner replied, "When I took a break, I sharpened my saw."

When we take breaks, we don't waste time, but we allow that time to sharpen our tools, rest, and rejuvenate so our energy can be replenished. To endure, we have to live like marathon runners and pace ourselves instead of like one-hundred-meter sprinters running a marathon. It just wouldn't work.

MORAL

Allowing time for the body to restore its energies and for maintenance of the tools we use helps us to work more efficiently.

Two Priests

The greatest step towards a life of simplicity is to learn
to let go.
> —Steve Maraboli, *Life, the Truth, and Being Free*

Two priests were walking through the woods. The young priest looked up to the older priest and was eager to learn from him as he embarked on his own journey to become the kind of spiritual leader his idol was.

As they walked through the forest, they came upon a stream. They saw that there was a young woman standing by it and she seemed to be lost in thought. She had a dilemma. She needed to get across to the other side of the stream but was afraid of slipping and falling. She also didn't want to get her clothes wet. The stream was wide, and the water looked turbulent as it flowed down over the slippery rocks.

As the priests came closer, she asked them to help her get across. While the younger priest hesitated, the older priest picked her up and walked cautiously through the stream, setting her down on the other side. She thanked them, and they walked on.

The young priest was unusually pensive. The older priest asked him what he was thinking. The young priest said, "I am confused by your action. We've taken vows of celibacy, and we aren't supposed to touch women. Why did you then carry that young woman across the stream?"

The older priest replied, "I set her down when I crossed the stream and left her there. Why are *you* still carrying her with you?"

Often in life, like the young priest, we carry people and situations with us for a long time and weigh ourselves down unnecessarily when those are best left behind for us to move forward.

MORAL

Dwelling on thoughts, feelings, or patterns that no longer serve us holds us back and keeps us from moving forward.

Holding His Finger

God is our refuge and strength, a very present help in trouble.

—Psalm 46:1 (King James Version)

Boarding schools, while providing a good education, can often be very challenging. It was even worse for me because the school I attended was in a different state. This meant that the language, foods, religion, and culture were very different from where I grew up. It was quite a transition from a public school to a private school. It was an all-girls Catholic school. While India encompasses many different religions and each state has its own language, English is the official language, and often the only common language.

When my parents dropped my sister and me at the school and left, we both felt quite lost initially. We were shy and took a while to make new friends. We had no one else to share our stories and experiences with. Every Sunday, we had to write letters to our parents. We also looked forward to getting letters from home. While these were helpful, they didn't make up for the lack of daily interaction that we'd had when we were home. I was feeling very depressed and lost. I wrote that to my father in one of the letters and insisted that since I was unhappy, I wanted to come home and go to a local school.

My father's reply to that eventually became a beacon of light, guiding me through many sticky situations in life while fostering a strong faith in the Almighty we call God.

Here is the gist of what Dad wrote:

- Your mom and I are making great sacrifices to send you to one of the best schools. While it feels uncomfortable for now, it will stand you in good stead as training to deal with life as you take on the world and deal with unforeseen situations in real life.
- Things won't always go your way; it's important that you learn to be grateful for what you have instead of crying for what you don't have.
- Always go through life, no matter where you are, holding His finger. This is the most important thing to remember. It will keep you from feeling lost and will provide support no matter where you are—whether you're with your earthly parents or not. For example, a child visiting Disneyland is holding his father's finger and walking with him. He is enjoying all the sights and having a great time. Suddenly, the child lets go of his father's finger and wanders off on his own. He realizes that his father is nowhere to be seen. He is afraid and lost without the only person he knows in this vast place. The sights, rides, and people are still around him, but he's no longer enjoying them because he's lost and afraid without that contact with his father. So, as you go through life and explore new vistas, do *not* let go of His finger!

MORAL

Just as an anchor keeps a boat from being adrift, having someone or something to hold on to keeps us safe from harm or getting lost.

Two Friends and a Horse

If treachery is the reward of trust, will the man who trusts come to harm?

—Mahatma Gandhi

Their friendship was legendary. They had been friends all their lives. Growing up as sons of the chiefs of neighboring villages, they shared a lot. They went to the same schools, and since they would eventually have similar responsibilities as chiefs after their fathers stepped down, their training for fulfilling those duties was also similar. However, there was always friendly rivalry and competitiveness between them where they tried to outdo each other in sports or other areas.

They both had stables that were well stocked with thoroughbreds and other fine horses. One of Ashok's horses was a beautiful white mare that was his pride and joy. She was elegant and regal, with a great personality, and Ashok loved her dearly. Raman coveted that beauty and would often ask Ashok to sell her to him. Ashok made it abundantly clear that she wasn't for sale.

As they went for their daily morning ride, Raman repeated his offer again. When Ashok refused again, Raman laughed and told Ashok that he was tired of asking him, so he was going to place a bet that he could get the mare one way or another before the week was out.

Upon hearing that, Ashok was worried and started to take extra precautions to make sure that Princess, his prize mare, would be safe in her stall. He could not sleep at night and would often get up and check the stall to make sure she was there. Raman teased him relentlessly about always being tired in the morning.

One morning as Ashok rode up to Raman's house to go on their morning ride, a servant informed him that Raman wasn't feeling well, so he wouldn't be going for the ride.

Ashok decided to go ahead alone. He could ride like the wind instead of just trotting as he normally did when riding with Raman, since they enjoyed talking during their leisurely ride. After an exhilarating gallop, Ashok was heading home and thinking that today was the last day of the week, and he still had his mare. He could now stop worrying about losing the mare and the bet. Lost in thought, he almost ran over a beggar on the roadside. He pulled up as he heard the beggar calling for help because he was cold and in a lot of pain. He could not walk any farther but needed to get to the village. Ashok pulled up and jumped off the mare. They weren't too far from the village now, so he would help the beggar get on the mare while he walked alongside, to take him where he needed to go. As the beggar struggled to get on the mare's back, Ashok held her and helped the beggar up.

Suddenly, the beggar snatched the reins from Ashok, and threw off the blanket that covered his face. As he rode off laughing, Ashok realized that it was Raman, posing as the beggar. Ashok was stunned.

Later in the day when they met again, Raman was very smug and pleased with himself about his victory. Ashok was feeling sad at the loss of his mare more than the bet. He asked just one thing of Raman. He knew that Raman had won the bet fair and square, but he asked that Raman not tell anyone how he won it. Raman teased him, "Are you embarrassed that I was able to steal the mare from right under your nose and win the bet?"

Ashok replied, "I'm not worried about losing the bet, but I am worried that if people find out how you tricked me by posing as a beggar, they'll stop helping anyone who needs help because they'll be afraid to trust them again."

Raman realized what the implications of his actions would be. He felt bad not only for deceiving his friend but also for causing people to mistrust the less fortunate who may need help. Although he was happy to have won the bet, he gave Ashok his mare back. They both remained friends for many more years and ruled their villages with compassion and kindness.

MORAL

When someone helps you but, in return, you cheat or trick that person, you take away that person's trust, so he or she fears to reach out and help others.

Angel to the Rescue

Sometimes angels are just ordinary people that help us
believe in miracles again.

—Anonymous

I was coming home from boarding school for the holidays. I was in
college now, so I had to learn to be more independent. Until now, I
had traveled to and from school with my parents or the nuns escorting
students to meeting points closest to our homes, from where the parents
would pick us up. This was the first time I'd have to make arrangements
myself for a taxi to take me to the bus stop in Simla, India, to travel to
Kalka, where my father was to meet me. Since it was the end of the term,
we also had to take home all our belongings—bedding in a hold-all, all
our clothes in a trunk, and miscellaneous toiletries in a small suitcase.

A day before we were to leave, when I called my father to coordinate
the time and meeting point, he asked me to travel by train instead of the
bus. He was dropping off my grandma at the railway station in Kalka as
she headed back home after her visit. He said that he could pick me up
from there when he dropped Grandma off.

I was ruffled because I had arranged for a taxi to take me to the bus
stand, which was closer to the college and I was more familiar with it. The
railway station was much farther, and so it would cost more. Besides, I
didn't know the train schedule and didn't know if I would be able to reach
Kalka in time to meet him. I wasn't comfortable dealing with all these

changes at the last minute. I figured that I would take the bus to Kalka and then take a cycle rickshaw to the train station.

All went well with my plan until the bus driver dropped me off at the Kalka bus stand. It was a small town, so the bus stand was more of a roadside stop. From there, I could see the railway station, and if it weren't for my luggage, I could have easily walked over.

The cycle rickshaw drivers saw my dilemma and knew that I couldn't very well walk with all my luggage, so they quoted a much higher rate than was justified for the short distance. I refused to pay that. I prepared to wait there, as my father would have to drive by there to get to the railway station. Even if he missed seeing me on the way to the station, he would see me on his way back when he didn't find me at the station.

As I stood and waited there, the rickshaw drivers talked loudly among themselves and jeered because I'd eventually have to get some sort of transportation as I couldn't lug the baggage anywhere.

I ignored them and said a silent prayer for protection. A few minutes later, a young gentleman dressed in white stopped by and asked if he could help. Somehow, I felt comfortable and trusted this man. He was courteous, respectful, kind, and helpful. When I explained the situation to him, he asked if there was someone he could call for me. Now, this was a time when very few people had telephones in their homes. They only had landlines in offices, and those also only for executives and senior officers. My parents did have a telephone at home, so when this gentleman said that he worked at the post office and could go there and call my father to inform him about my situation, I gave him my number. He left to make the call. He came back a few minutes later to let me know that my father would stop by and pick me up from the bus stand. He also told me that he would wait there with me to make sure I was safe.

He stood very respectfully a few feet behind me. The jeering comments from across the road stopped. Those drivers glanced at me periodically but said nothing. I saw some confusion and a kind of awe in their glances.

About an hour later, my father drove up and pulled over by me to let me know that he will drop off my grandma and then be back to pick me up, as then there will be room in the car for me and my luggage.

When he came back, he and my mom grilled me about the guy who'd called them. I gave them the gist of the situation and put my luggage in the trunk of the car with Dad's help.

Before getting in the car, I turned around to thank the gentleman, who I thought was still standing behind me, but there was no one. My father had not seen anyone standing behind me at all.

I was confused at first. Then, as I thought more about it, I started to notice some oddities that I had not realized before.

In those days, phone calls were expensive and even family and friends who knew you would hesitate to let you use their phones to avoid incurring big charges. This gentleman had offered to make the long distance call from the post office where he worked. Phones were used for business only, not for personal use without consequences. And finally, it was Sunday: the post office was closed.

Yes, in hindsight, I recognize that my guardian angel had been there to protect me.

MORAL

There are guardian angels and helpful people who cross paths with you when you need them. All you have to do is ask with the faith of a child who knows his parents will take care of him, even if sometimes you don't believe in them.

Spirits Send Help!

Make yourself familiar with the angels, and behold them frequently in Spirit, for without being seen, they are present with you.

—St. Francis of Sales

I had been having health issues that weren't responding to medication. It was now at the point where the surgery my doctor had suggested wasn't an option anymore; it was necessary.

My husband and I discussed our finances, because even with insurance, the co-pay for the doctor fees and hospital bills would be sizeable. We'd taken some hits with our business, and a one-week stay in the hospital following surgery wouldn't be cheap, so it was a major concern.

To prepare for that, we called the insurance company and were assured that all was good. They would pay 80 percent of both the doctor's fee and the hospital bill, and we would have to pay 20 percent per the terms of our policy.

After the surgery when I came home, we called to follow up with the insurance company about how and where to submit the bills. We were shocked to find out that the insurance company had gone under and would no longer pay any of the bills. Overnight, we were liable for the entire 100 percent of all the bills.

We were certainly not prepared for this expense, but it was what it was. We called the hospital to explain the situation and negotiate monthly payments after making a down payment. The gentleman we spoke with was very helpful, and we settled on the amount we would need to pay per month until the balance was paid in full. The 20 percent we'd budgeted was used to pay the doctor's fee in full, so that helped.

After we'd sent in our second payment to the hospital, we got a call from one of their representatives, demanding payment in full. When I explained about the negotiated payments, he said that the person we'd made the arrangement with wasn't authorized to do so and, if we didn't pay the full balance within the week, they would take us to court. With everything that was going on, in addition to my painful recovery, I was overwhelmed. That night, when I couldn't sleep, I got down on my knees, and with tears streaming down my face, I asked God why all this was happening. After all, we were working hard to earn an honest living and trying to do the right thing but were falling deeper and deeper into the hole. I pleaded for help.

After that I lay down in bed again. I must have fallen asleep, because I recall being woken up by a presence in my room. With my eyes half open, I felt that this presence was greater than me and that I could not receive it lying down. I had to sit up out of respect. When I opened my eyes, I saw a huge, pale-gold ball of shimmering light from floor to ceiling. It felt very comforting. I just knew that things would be okay. I didn't ask how, when, why, or where, but I knew I didn't need to worry about it any longer. I lay down again and slept like a baby, wrapped in its warmth.

When I woke up the next day, I felt very lighthearted.

About a week after my experience, I was at work in our retail store, helping a customer, when the new salesgirl came to ask me the price of a dress that another customer was inquiring about. The dress was from a recently arrived shipment that I had not tagged yet. I asked her to help my customer, and I went to help the other lady.

As I approached her, she put back the dress she was holding, pointed at me and said, "You! You're the one. You have been asking the Spirits for help. They have sent me to help you!"

It had been a week since my experience, I was now at work and in a different mindset, so while a part of my brain listened to her, in the other part, I questioned myself, wondering what she was talking about. While she was telling me things about me that no one else would know, to validate what she was saying, a part of me was going along with what she was telling me. She assured me that everything would work out.

A few days later, I learned that a family friend who is an attorney was going to help us handle the case at a greatly discounted rate.

The hospital filed a case against us, but on the day of the court date, no one from the hospital showed up, so our attorney was able to negotiate a greatly reduced settlement!

MORAL

There are forces in the universe that surround us and are always ready to help, if only we know and ask for their help. Knowing that we attract to us what we are, we learn to encourage only positive thoughts and let only positive people surround us.

Spirits Send Help 2

A few days after my experience in the shop with the lady who was sent by the spirits to help me, I went to see her at her place to find out more and figure out some more messages.

That evening she told me many more things about me that she couldn't have known, since these were told to me by astrologers and numerologists in India about my recent and distant past, as far back as some past lives.

Then she proceeded to tell me that she saw some danger to me and my family, but she couldn't see exactly what it was. She asked for my address so she could pray for protection and ask the angels to guard us. While a part of me doubted her, I gave her the address. I left that night trying to figure out why I had done that and why I was complying while questioning it and not understanding much of it.

That night as I sat watching TV in the family room, while my husband and children slept, I was still thinking about it.

During a scary scene in the movie, I thought I heard a sound from the garage. As I looked up, I saw the garage door open into the house, and a man stepped inside. I froze. I thought my husband had gone to bed. Was he working in the garage? I ran to the bedroom. My husband lay sleeping in the bed. I shook him and woke him up. As he sat up, half-awake, I told him that there was a man in our house. I dialed 911 while he collected his thoughts. Then he ran out in the hall, banging on the walls and shouting to scare the intruder. Before we were married, when my husband had lived by the beach with his buddies, someone had broken into their house. The police had then advised them to never confront the intruder as he could have a gun, but to make a noise to let him know they were awake. This would scare him, as generally, the intruder is there to steal some money to support his drug habit.

However, this person was so sure that I was alone and making that noise that he still kept walking in. When he and my husband saw each other around the corner, they both turned back and ran—he ran out of the house, and my husband ran back to the bedroom.

I was still on the phone with the 911 operator, explaining what the noise was about. Our bedroom window was at an angle where we could see the main road. My husband saw the man walking as if nothing had happened. He had a description of the person and what he wore. We were able to give that to the police. Fortunately, it was a slow night for them, so two patrol cars and a helicopter tracked the intruder, and they were able to arrest him.

Police got plenty of fingerprints from the garage. Apparently, he had slipped in while we had the front door propped open partially with a fan for some cross ventilation on a hot evening.

It turned out that he was the serial rapist who had been going around in the neighborhood for the last couple of months, asking to use the phone, saying that his truck had broken down. When allowed inside, he'd then raped the women. I remembered someone had come to my door about a week before, asking to use the phone. Our house was on the corner of a main road, and we would normally let people use our phone if there was an accident or if someone's vehicle had broken down. This was before the cell phone era! But since we'd been notified about the serial rapist, I was cautious. This one day while I was alone at home, my doorbell had rang, and there he was, asking to use the phone because his truck had broken down. I had the chain on the door, and I refused to let him in, saying that there was a gas station a little farther down. He became angry and started yelling at me, so I closed the door. It turned out that he had been watching me since then. We also found his footprints outside the kitchen window.

As I reflected on the incident, I realized what a narrow escape we'd all had. The children slept through the whole commotion. The guy was in my house! He could have had a gun! He could have done anything. That is when I remembered what the lady had told me about sending the angels to guard the house. They sure had.

Her name was Sister Sophia. She helped me a lot for many years after that, with many decisions, energy clearing, karmic situations, and so on. She would often show up when I had questions that desperately needed answers but when I could not reach her by phone or get to her place to talk to her.

After her work was done, she went out of my life as suddenly as she had appeared. Although I don't know where she is, or if she has transitioned, I say a silent prayer of thanks to the Spirits who sent her and to her for appearing when she did.

Note: When this incident happened, I had just started reading *The Third Eye* by Lobsang Rampa. This is a book about the author's life in Tibet. In that book, he states that, in Tibet, criminals weren't put in jails, but in chains, and left on the streets to beg for their food. He goes on to say that everyone knew they were criminals, but they were kind to them because they realized that, but for a stroke of luck, it could be them. Everyone has broken the law sometime or the other, ranging from a minor infraction to a major crime. These people just were caught while we were not.

When I was notified about the date for the intruder's hearing so I could be there if I wanted to, I chose instead to send a letter. I don't know if he ever got it and read it. I didn't remember his face. In the letter, I told him so, and I said that I would choose not to look for him in every stranger that I walked by. Even though he knew where I lived and what I looked like, I would never know him. However, I choose to forgive him, but I wouldn't live in fear of him. I shared the story from the book and suggested that, whatever he had been or done so far with his life, he would now have an opportunity to reflect on his choices and decide to change the course of his life. I don't know where he is or what he chose to do, but I set myself free that day.

MORAL

Sometimes when bad things happen, they are either lessons for us to learn, for the other person to learn, or simply tests of our faith. Staying positive and forgiving as we seek forgiveness in such cases is very important.

Portraits of Good and Evil

> Watch your thoughts, they become your words; watch your words, they become your actions; watch your actions, they become your habits; watch your habits, they become your character; watch your character, it becomes your destiny.
>
> — Lao Tzu

Once there was an artist who wanted to paint a portrait that would embody all that was good, so he decided to look for a model who would exude the qualities in looks that people could relate to. His model would need to have a beautiful face with kind eyes, a gentle smile, and a loving demeanor, with an inner glow that lit up his face. He traveled vast distances in search of the perfect model. Finally, he found one in a small town. This young man had all the qualities that the artist was looking for, so he made a deal with him, took some pictures, and went home to start his work.

It took him a long time to paint the picture exactly as he wanted it. It was a labor of love, and the picture did justice to what the artist wanted to represent. When he was satisfied with his work, he decided to work on the other painting representing evil.

For this portrait, he went to look for his model in a prison near a very rough part of the city. He looked at thieves, robbers, and murderers. He found a young man who looked so evil that even the artist wasn't sure that he had the courage to approach him to discuss his plan. Eventually, he built up the courage and went to meet him, offered him money, and sought his permission to use his image to represent evil as part of his two-portrait set.

While there, he was curious to know what kind of life this young man had experienced to make him what he was. He hesitantly asked his questions. As they talked, he found that the young man, unlike his reputation, was soft-spoken and answered his questions quite willingly. When the artist asked why he was opening up to him about his bad choices and evil actions, the young man told him that it was because the artist had been kind to him before. The artist looked confused because he didn't remember ever meeting him before. The young man reminded him that they had met when the artist was looking for a model for his first portrait. He was the model that the artist had used for his first portrait.

The artist was very surprised and asked him, "So how did you go on to become who you are today from who you were when I first met you? You had everything going for you. What happened?"

The young man went on to talk about his journey. He said that he didn't pay attention to the small choices, but made some bad ones. He got mixed up with the wrong crowd to be popular. He forgot to have fun in simple ways but chose the excitement of accepting "dares," slowly landing him in trouble more frequently at school, and he let his grades drop. As he spiraled, he became depressed but didn't know how to get out of this whirlpool. He didn't retrace his steps or seek help as he saw this as a sign of weakness. Instead, he became more defiant. To keep up the false bravado, as he sank deeper and deeper, he started doing drugs, stealing from his parents to support his habit and lying to them.

Eventually as he grew taller and physically stronger than his aging parents, he even threatened them. Finally, he ran away from home to get to a big city that would offer more opportunities to support his new lifestyle. He started selling drugs and eventually committed murder. He found that he needed higher doses of the drugs to quell the slowly fading voice of his conscience, and he managed to almost kill his soul. When he was eventually arrested, he saw himself as a victim of circumstance and still didn't take responsibility for his part in the making of this new him.

It was only now when he saw the artist and recalled his simple life, filled with love and joy that he retraced his steps to his own door.

* * *

Remember that when you hit rock bottom, you can only go up. You can make that climb, if you stop seeing yourself as a victim or if you stop blaming others or circumstances. We always have the option to respond differently to whatever life throws at us. If you fall ten times, get up eleven times. Be patient with yourself, but don't waiver in your intention. If you fail, forgive yourself and try again. Seek help. Choose supportive people. Accept their help in pulling you out of this quagmire, but don't try to pull them down into it with you. Love yourself. Acknowledge your mistakes, for only then can you be motivated to correct them. Choose companions on your journey who will walk with you and lift you up when you stumble, who will keep you on the straight and narrow when you deviate from your path and give you tough love. You don't need those who will mock you or encourage you to "do your own thing" to keep you where they are only to justify their choices and to keep you as a customer for what they are selling. You have a choice.

MORAL

Beware the lure of the path of least resistance, for it will lead you to a very crooked road where you may find it difficult to make your way back.

PART 2

How to Do It

In part 1, you learned what you need to do. In part 2, there are suggestions for how to do it. These are helpful tools to get you where you want to go, but the journey is yours. How successful you are at doing this will depend on how committed you are to your goals and how much effort you're willing to put into it. Sometimes taking that first step is the most difficult part. Once you do that and see the small changes that begin to clear your path, you're encouraged to keep going.

When people are so unhappy with their current situations that they decide to make concerted efforts to change it, they look for ways to do it. This intention brings to them the information they need to fulfill that desire. So you must be ready to make the change, which is why you have been led to this book.

Taking responsibility and not blaming other people or circumstances for your troubles is the first step. Not only does it put you on the right path, but also it empowers you to take action.

Although there are many books for you to choose from to learn how to do what you need to do to change your life, continue to grow and be the best version of yourself that you're capable of being, I have chosen to share the following four books with you. In these books, you'll find very basic and easy ways to identify what you need to change, why you should change, and how to change.

If you find that these books don't resonate with you, there are many others that you may connect with, so choose what works for you. There's no limit to the ways change can be brought about, so travel on with companions of your choosing. Remember: life is a journey, not a destination. When you hit a plateau, rest for a bit, but don't give up.

May the Angels Be with You

Gary Quinn

I n this book, Gary Quinn shares his experience with us about how archangel Michael appeared to him at Notre Dame Cathedral in Paris, France. He goes on to explain how we also can tap into the power of the angels and get help from them whether we believe in them or not. He tells us about various angels, how they operate, what their work is, and how to invoke their help. He also teaches us about ways to access our spirit guides and create the lives we want.

How much success we have in invoking the help of the angels depends on how positive or negative our attitude is, whether we're disciplined enough to get out of our own way, or if we can differentiate between the messages we receive from the angels or if our own egos take over. To have the best experience, you need to ask and then allow it to be without placing time limits or looking for what you think the answer should be or how it should come to you. Sometimes it's so subtle that you totally miss it. Other times it's so clear that you can have absolutely no doubts.

SOME EXCERPTS FROM THE BOOK

> Letting go of our defenses is frightening at first—but ultimately it is such a relief! I urge you to try to release your fear and anger every chance you get, especially

any moment you feel yourself clench and about to say, "But ..." Allow whatever feeling, thought, or opinion occurs to you simply to be. Just "hear" it. Don't argue or attempt to explain it away. Don't do anything about it! Simply make room for whatever thoughts come after it. Entertain each of your thoughts like guests. Be courteous, withhold judgement, just keep the flow going. Eventually it will become clear to you which "guests" feel welcome (or "true"). You will be clearing your psychic airwaves—not only to allow truth to reveal and prove itself, but also to open up the path for your angels.

Of course, if truth were always so easy to perceive and acknowledge, a lot more would be self-evident. Certainly, if the truth about angels came to us more frequently in physically or conventionally identifiable ways, we wouldn't have consigned them to Christmas decorations or wishful sitcoms. We would acknowledge them openly in our lives as very real presences.

Living in the Spiritual Zone

Gary Quinn

T his is a book about ten clearly defined and easy-to-follow steps to change your life and discover your truth.

Gary shows us how in three parts:

1. *How to Get to the Spiritual Zone*

   You will need to use your imagination and insight to become aware of your own truth. Understanding yourself and practicing being honest with yourself in that discovery will help you move forward. To open yourself to receiving the love that you deserve will require a lot of letting go of the past and forgiving yourself and others.

2. *How to Stay in the Spiritual Zone*

   Once you get there, how to stay there will be the next lesson to learn. In order to do that, you'll have to activate your power of choice and determine what are the better choices for you. Recognizing that you have support and reprogramming yourself to change old patterns will make you feel comfortable in this new environment. "The more we allow our spiritual truth to flow freely through us, the more we make ourselves available to the surprising and miraculous gifts that our spirituality provides."[2]

3. *How to Manifest in the Spiritual Zone*
    Finally, once you have learned how to get there and stay there, you will learn how to *manifest* in the spiritual zone. You will recognize yourself as a creator, visualizing the life you want, enjoying spiritual financial freedom while living in service. You will learn that "giving" is a way to make room for "receiving."

With simple techniques, insightful questions, and wise suggestions, he guides us through this maze.

SOME EXCERPTS FROM THE BOOK

> The pull of materialism brings with it inherent dissatisfactions: we have lost touch, literally with the earth. Think about how often does your skin touch soil? ... Today, we feign a connectedness to the whole of life, trying to pretend that our broadband hook-up to the World Wide Web is itself meaningful. Yes, we can e-mail friends and strangers anywhere in the world within a matter of seconds. Sure, this is a fantastic tool—but how many times, honestly, has it enriched your spiritual life?

> Our bodies are the temples of our spirits. If we don't feed the right things to our bodies, we won't be in alignment to stay tuned and receive the messages and guidance we need. We also won't have the energy and stamina to do the work we are here to do.

---

[2] Gary Quinn, *Living in the Spiritual Zone* (Deerfield Beach: Health Communications, 2005), xvii.

We are, right now, in a major shift in human consciousness. All humanity is stepping out of darkness and into the light of the Spiritual Zone. For thousands of years, people have been living in their defensive egos, separate from spirit and separate from truth. Now we are beginning to realize that in truth, we are all spiritual beings. We are all one spiritual being. Our home is the Zone. Our egos, however, will never accept this: they are innately separate, defensive constructs, and as such unable to trust. Do we identify with them, as we have habitually and historically done, or do we listen to the call and acknowledge and accept our true spiritual selves? This is the grand struggle of our present era. Do we step into the Zone, or do we remain in illusion? Our journey will inevitably lead to our eventual transcendence for truth always overcomes illusion. But just because it is inevitable doesn't mean we always make it easy on ourselves.

The Yes Frequency

Gary Quinn

Gary teaches us how to "master a positive belief system and achieve mindfulness."

Stand with your head held high and your arms stretched up, forming a Y, and let the frequency, spirit, energy, and power of *yes* infuse your body, mind, and soul.

In this book, he explains the various frequencies and how we can tap into those:

1. *Taking Control of Your Life*

   Tuning into "the Yes Frequency," "the Forgiving Frequency," and "the Self-Love Frequency" take you to the next level of taking control of your life. You will learn how to find your way, take responsibility, and let go of fear and self-sabotage. You will also be more confident and know the power of surrender to love and having gratitude.

2. *Reconfigure Your Behavior*

   To reconfigure your behavior, and to purify your frequency, you will need to let go of your attachment to negative behavior, eliminate anger, master your emotions, and enjoy the positive use of meditation.

You will learn how improving the frequency of your words will empower you. You will learn to overcome negative self-talk, learn to trust and sustain your self-confidence.

3. *Living Your Vision*
   If you follow the steps above, you will be ready to tackle the intuition frequency and success frequency. You will be on your way to step into the process, receive information and build your ideal life with visualization.

SOME EXCERPTS FROM THE BOOK

There is a frequency that surrounds us. It vibrates life into all aspects of the universe. When you understand how to engage your frequency, your life will plug into abundance, success, and contentment.

People all over the world have changed their lives, just by repeating the word YES. I have no idea why it works—I don't ask, I just trust, because I have seen it work wondrous transformations.

While it's important to look at our mistakes and find ways to make improvements, it isn't in our spiritual, emotional, physical, or psychological best interest to use these mistakes as an excuse to put ourselves down.

Gary Quinn is a life coach, television host, television producer, and an intuitive who works with angelic forces. He is the founder of the Touchstone for Life Coaching Certification Program and the Angelic Intervention Coaching Program.

He is also an international bestselling author and works at Gary Quinn Productions and *Energie Magazine*. You can follow him on Facebook and Twitter.

Breakthrough Moments: 5 Step Formula for Getting Out of Your Own Way and Having the Life You Love

Suzie Emiliozzi

In this book, Suzie Emiliozzi tells you about the five easy steps that can help you break out of the dismal place that you find yourself stuck in. If you're ready and willing to make the changes to move to a better place for a better life, then this will guide you to do so in simple and easy to incorporate ways. By moving out of your own way, you can have the kind of life you want.

You will learn how to shift into a new perspective by giving yourself permission and exploring the possibilities. You will be on your way to becoming a powerful authority by giving it your purposeful attention. You will also be ready for self-care and able to get out of a funk if you're willing to put in the work.

SOME EXCERPTS FROM THE BOOK

Often the problems and hurts in life feel bigger than the self; it can feel like being at the mercy of the experience *du jour*. There is a sense of powerlessness, stuck-ness, victimization, lack of control, and more. In the thick of that experience, it is easy to forget the extraordinary nature of you. It's easy to forget that you're a powerful being, capable of great things. It's easy to forget that you are the director of your life. It is important to know that you can focus your attention and energy in such a way that things change—easily and quickly. Choose to remember (or now know) that you are extraordinary.

We are very creative beings so we can come up with many ways to stand between ourselves and our potential. We often hold ourselves back from experiencing the heart's desires by requiring permission from self, others or God/Source/Spirit before we can move forward. Asking, "Why do I feel this way? Why is this so?" are not helpful questions to resolve inner conflict. Instead, claim permission. Claiming permission sets us free from old, binding chains and opens the door to change.

Suzie Emiliozzi, RN, CBP, CHt is a healer, author, coach. Having studied many approaches to healing and change, Suzie's work evolved into a comprehensive program that includes techniques based in spirituality, ancient wisdom, psychology, philosophy, the modern sciences, and her own modality: BLISS.

For more information on her various services, you can check out Suzie's website—www.suzieemiliozzi.com.

PART 3

Inspirational Thoughts and Quotes

Philosophical Ramblings of the Heart

On the following pages, I share some of the ramblings of my heart. Use these to guide you when you feel lost, support you when you feel you can no longer go on, or to uplift you when you're feeling down. Add some of your own that you connect with. Read these often. Depending on where you're in your life and what you're going through at that moment, these will remind you that you're not alone and to see the light at the end of the tunnel. Others have been there and gotten through tough times. You can too!

A Mother's Dilemma

Give her a few moments of peace, my Lord.
My child is very sad and lonely.
Let her feel my love, my God.
In her own world of thoughts, she is lonely.
How can I break the walls and bring her out, my Lord?
Locked in her own heart, she is lonely.
Tell me how I can share her pain, my God.
Having surrounded herself with dark nights, she is lonely.
I am standing at her door with a lamp in my hand, my Lord,
But she is sitting behind the door, and she is lonely.
Either give me the key to that door,
Or give me the strength to break that door,
Or give her the courage to come into the light,
And also let her realize, my God,
That without her, I am lonely.

Dark to Light

She stood there, so lonely and afraid.
Life was crumbling around her.
All that she had ever known,
was slowly disintegrating—oh, ever so slowly.
The walls she had built around her heart
to protect herself from the world
of hurt and hate were dropping,
leaving her vulnerable and exposed.
She stood frozen in fear as the first rays of light penetrated,
now breaking the walls of her dark and dank
prison cell of locked emotions
that she was afraid to face.
With the light came a breath of
fresh air and the ever-widening
opening letting in the cleansing rain.
Being exposed to the elements that
she feared, she allowed herself
to gingerly step out into the light
and air and rain—the life-giving
elements she had hidden from
because she was afraid of letting go,
of appearing weak, of being vulnerable.

But lo and behold! The rain of tears
cleansed her heart of debris.
The air of openness gave her new life!
In a few moments she had gone from
dark to light!

Resolved

And the light of knowledge gave her courage to hold her head high
And walk into the light, to breathe the air and to smile up in the rain.
She walked away from the dark, dingy and now crumbling prison walls,
with her head held high,
And her spirit lifted and her soul challenged.
She had found herself.
She was learning to love herself.
She was ready to fly.
She had arrived!

Who Am I?

Who am I?
You asked me who I am.
I was silenced for
How do I begin to answer such a vast question?
I am body. I am soul. I am young. I am old.
I am lover. I am strife.
I am mother. I am child. I am sister. I am wife.
I am neighbor. I am friend.
I am who I am till the end.
I am …

My Power

I am the sun that lights the world.
I am the clouds in the sky.
I am the flight of the birds.
I hold the entire universe in me.
I am power
Until I fear myself and give my power away.

Random Thoughts

No matter how many times you're right, examine your actions and how you come across when someone's being unreasonable and aggressive toward you to make sure that you didn't inadvertently step on his or her toes without realizing or meaning to. *No* isn't always negative, and *yes* isn't always positive. Understand the difference.

In life, we constantly meet the same situation, albeit in different garbs—something that we need to overcome. It's only when we learn to rise above it that we're ready to move on. They celebrated when I was born. Did I live a life that justified that celebration?

You always get what you expect, consciously or unconsciously. That's why it is so important to watch your thoughts. Meditate more, so you'll have to medicate less.

When we take, take, take, we leave the person/resource incomplete and unbalanced. When we give, give, give, we leave ourselves incomplete and unbalanced. When we give and take, give and take, give and take, we strike a balance, we're productive, and we all grow.

You're either here or there. Remember to be here and present in your life. You're either grateful or not.

Remember to be grateful for your life and all it brings you and all that it represents—even if you feel you don't have enough, don't do enough, or aren't enough. Be grateful anyway for your life and all that it has provided. Either you appreciate it, or you don't. Remember to appreciate what you have received instead of complaining about what you have not. It lets the givers know that you like what you have received and encourages them to give more. If you only complain, you discourage them from reaching out again.

It's said that truth is stranger than fiction. That is so because fiction has to fit in the mold of what we know or what we've heard, seen, or experienced to be believable. Truth, on the other hand, has no such limits.

People who follow the path of least resistance, like a river, also become crooked like the river and cause much destruction.

When your body gets dirty, you wash it with soap and water. You don't throw it away. When your heart, mind, soul, or spirit becomes tainted with bad thoughts, lust, and greed, you clean those with love, positive thoughts, prayers, and positive actions.

The optimist says the glass is half-full. The pessimist says the glass is half-empty. They are both right! But also remember: whether the glass is half-full or half-empty, it is refillable.

An acorn has the potential and the power to be an oak tree, but it isn't that yet. It hasn't developed that potential, has not experienced growth that will totally shatter its existence as the seed that it is now, or the pain of losing its current identity to become stronger, bigger and venture on its journey. There are so many acorns that remain as they are, fall from the tree, and do not develop their innate powers, yet they serve in that capacity as food for squirrels and other small animals. Similarly, no life is wasted. It's just utilized in a different capacity.

It's very important to understand oneself. It's just as important to love oneself. It's even more important to acknowledge that you're lovable and you deserve to be loved.

Remember: being lovable doesn't mean you're perfect. It just means that while you have faults and failings, you're not a failure, and you're worthy of love and still deserve to be loved.

Respect yourself! In your own small way, you make a valid and worthy contribution to society. You weren't born to be merely a headline for tomorrow or to cause pain and grief to those around you.

Learn where you fit in and what you contribute. Each contribution matters. Don't underestimate your contribution no matter how small. By the same token, don't inflate your ego if your contribution is large.

If books aren't read but are buried under dust and debris for many years, it will take a lot of time and effort to bring them out, dust them, and restore them to a readable state. The dust mites and other bugs will cause discomfort and allergies to flare up. Find ways to minimize discomfort. One way would be to sprinkle some water on the dust to settle it, but that would damage the books. Wearing masks to keep from inhaling dust particles will help. Once cleaned up, it would be wise to read the books or the cleanup effort will have been wasted. You might as well have saved yourself the trouble if you were just going to let them sit for years again to collect dust.

When we're ready to change our circumstances and negative habits acquired over the years, we know that it will take time and dedicated effort to do so. By the time we get to a place that could be the launching pad to greatness, often we're either too tired or too afraid to do that. So we just sit, make excuses and do nothing.

Trust yourself. Trust the process. Trust the universe. It has brought you here. It will take you further too. This isn't the time to hibernate but to act. Fly!

Accepting help isn't a sign of weakness. Giving help doesn't mean you own the receiver's soul.

No one should be grateful at the cost of his or her self-respect. Developing a sense of self-worth is worth the effort.

There is nothing as strong as gentleness, and there is nothing as gentle as real strength.

Choose what stories you listen to. Choose what kind of people you surround yourself with.

Don't judge others for their choices but also don't take on the burden of their choices.

When things seem to be out of control, remember you still have a choice to respond, not react.

INSPIRATIONAL WORDS OF WISDOM

Poems, Stories, and Quotes

After a While

So, plant your own garden and decorate your own soul,
instead of waiting for someone to bring you flowers.
And you learn that you can endure …
That you are strong,
And you do have worth.

—Author Unknown

A Sense of a Goose

Finally—and this is important—when a goose gets sick
or is wounded by gunshot and falls out of formation, two
other geese fall out with that goose and follow it down to
lend help and protection. They stay with the fallen goose
until it is able to fly or until it dies; and only then do they
launch out on their own, or with another formation to
catch up with their group.

If we have the sense of a goose, we will stand by each
other like that.

—Author Unknown

A Life Worth Saving

A man risked his life by swimming through the
treacherous riptide to save a youngster being swept out
to sea. After the child recovered from the harrowing
experience, he said to the man, "Thank you for saving
my life."

The man looked into the boy's eyes and said, "That's
okay, kid. Just make sure your life was worth saving."

—Author Unknown

147

Note: Although the man's response seems harsh, it is in fact very wise. He is asking the boy to make sure that he makes something of his life, so the man's effort in saving him wasn't wasted (e.g., if the boy goes on to commit crimes or gets involved in other unlawful activities instead of living a worthy and productive life).

> Raat bhar ka hai mehman andhera
> Kiske rokai ruka hai savera

Translation:
Darkness is merely a guest of the night
Who has been able to stop the morning?

—Couplet from a Bollywood song

> Zarre zarre mein usi ka noor hai
> Jhaank khud mein woh na tujhse door hai
> Ishq hai us se toh sabse ishq kar
> Is Ibadat ka yahi dastoor hai

Translation:
In every speck shines His Divine light
Look within yourself, He isn't far from you
If you love Him, then love everyone
This is the way of this worship.

—Unknown

> Vani mein bhi ajeeb shakti hoti hai ...
> Kadwa bolne wale ka shahad bhi nahin bikta
> Meettha bolne wale ki mirch bhi bik jaati hai

Translation:
The voice has a strange power
He who speaks in a rude tone, cannot even sell honey
Yet he who speaks in a sweet tone can even sell chilies.

—Unknown

A smart person knows what to say.
A wise person knows whether to say it or not.

—Dalai Lama

A person who is always right usually gets left.

—Unknown

If you wish to understand yourself, see how others act.
If you wish to understand others, look in your own heart.

—Unknown

Like a procession you walk together towards your god-self.
You are the way and the wayfarers.
And when one of you falls down, he falls for those behind him, a caution against stumbling stone.
Ay, and he falls for those ahead of him, who though faster and surer of foot, yet removed not the stumbling stone.

—Kahlil Gibran, *The Prophet*

Are you doing yourselves justice when you lift your eyes towards Almighty God and call him Father, and then turn around, bow your heads before a man and call him Master?
Are you contented, as sons of god, with being slaves of man? Did not Christ call you brethren?

—Kahlil Gibran, *Spirits Rebellious*

Courage is the fear that has said her prayers.

—Sarah Ban Breathnach, *Simple Abundance*

Better keep yourself clean
And bright; you are the
Window through which you must
see the world.

—George Bernard Shaw

Worry is not a conscious act of creative thinking that intends to find solutions to a concern rather it is a dead thought loop that can become the subliminal background music of an unconscious mind. It is nonetheless creative—*unconsciously manifesting negativity into our lives.*

—Gary Quinn, *Living in the Spiritual Zone*

Forgiveness corrects your very human mistake of identifying with the limited mind and realigns you with the unlimited spiritual being you truly are. You will find that as you release your tight hold on your perceived limits, you will relax into the ready flow of your abundant spirituality.

—Gary Quinn, *Living in the Spiritual Zone*

Do not speak so much that people wait for you to be silent.
Speak just enough before being silent, that people wait for you to speak again.

—President A.P.J. Abdul Kalam
(translated from a quote)

If I keep silent, it is for a reason
You surely know I have the power to speak?

—Mirza Ghalib, translation from couplet

When you have more than enough, build a longer table not a higher fence.

—Unknown

The one who plants trees, knowing he will never sit in their shade, has at least started to understand the meaning of life.

—Rabindranath Tagore

It is easier to say what we believe than be what we believe.

—Dr. Robert Anthony, *Think Again*

If you think something outside of yourself is the cause of your problem, you will look outside of yourself for the answer.

—Dr. Robert Anthony, *Think Again*

What is, was
What was, is
What will be, is up to me.

Dr. Robert Anthony, *Think Again*

Is there anyone so wise as to learn by the experience of others?

Voltaire

Do not look back in anger or forward in fear, but around in awareness.

James Thurber

Character cannot be developed in ease and quiet. Only through experiences of trial and suffering can the soul be strengthened, vision cleared, ambition inspired and success achieved.

—Helen Keller

The marvelous richness of human experience would lose something of rewarding joy if there were no limitations to overcome. The hilltop hour would not be half so wonderful if there were no dark valleys to traverse.

—Helen Keller

If you could treat an individual ... as if he were what he ought to be and could be, he will become what he ought to be and could be.

—Goethe

And life is what we make it, always has been, always will be.

—Grandma Moses

Those who wish to sing always find a song.

—Swedish proverb

I am only one. But still, I am one. I cannot do everything, but still I can do something. And because I cannot do everything, I will not refuse to do the something that I can do.

—Edward Everett Hale

The heart of a fool is in his mouth, but the mouth of a wise man is in his heart.

—Benjamin Franklin

When you take a bowl in your hand and go begging to the Lord, you receive a bowlful. But when you seek to receive His blessing with all the love in your heart, then what you receive is limitless.

—Unknown

God has the power to heal your legs, so you can walk again. Do not use Him merely as a crutch. Recognize the strength and power of His blessings completely and ask Him to make you whole instead of merely providing you with something to lean on. Thus, you become His image with His powers to create. Use these wisely. Let

your heart guide your soul. Be careful not to let your ego
slip in the driver's seat. It is a better servant than a master.

—Unknown

Most of the problems in life come because of two reasons:
We act without thinking, and
We keep thinking without acting.

—Unknown

Make sure your worst enemy is not living between your
ears.

—Thinking Humanity Group

A good relationship is when someone accepts your past,
supports your present and encourages your future.

—Unknown

Do not build walls, but learn to transcend them.

—Joan Brady, *God on a Harley*

Live in the moment for each one is precious and not to
be squandered.

—Joan Brady, *God on a Harley*

Men are four:
He who knows not, and knows not he knows not, he is a
fool, shun him.
He who knows not, and knows he knows not, he is simple,
teach him.
He who knows, and knows not he knows, he is asleep,
wake him.
He who knows, and knows he knows, he is wise,
follow him.

—Unknown

Your career is what you are paid for
Your calling is what you are made for

—Steve Harvey

The one who loves you will never leave you, because even
if there are 100 reasons to give up, he/she will find one
reason to hold on.

—Ratan Tata

There is difference between a "human being" and "being
human."

—Ratan Tata

If you want to walk fast—
Walk alone.
If you want to walk far—
Walk together.

—Ratan Tata

Six Best Doctors in the World:

1. Sunlight
2. Rest
3. Exercise
4. Diet
5. Self Confidence and
6. Friends

Maintain them in all stages of life and you will enjoy a
healthy life.

—Ratan Tata

Conclusion

In conclusion, know the following:

- Resources are available and helpers are all around you.
- You have the power. If you have surrendered it for some reason, take it back and be a victim no more.
- Be patient with yourself. Forgive yourself and others.
- In life, there are positives and negatives. Find your balance and be grateful for all you have instead of being fearful for what you *may* not have.
- Taking action or making excuses is the choice you will need to make.
- How long will you continue to be a victim? In life, sometimes you're the hammer that strikes at the anvil, and at other times you're the anvil that is stricken by the hammer. Find the balance and be ready to strike when it is your turn to be the hammer.
- While giving is commendable, learning to receive gracefully is also advisable. It means you have learned to set aside your ego and have accepted your humanness.

Suggested Reading

Brady, Joan. *God on a Harley.* Old Tappan, NJ: Simon & Schuster, 1995.

Brand, Russell. *Recovery: Freedom from Our Addictions.* New York: Henry Holt, 2017.

Breathnach, Sarah Ban. *Simple Abundance: A Daybook of Comfort and Joy.* New York: Warner Books, 1995.

Breathnach, Sarah Ban. *Something More: Excavating Your Authentic Self.* New York: Warner Books, 1998.

Brooks, David. *The Road to Character.* New York: Random House, 2015.

Brown, Brene. *The Gifts of Imperfection.* Center City, MN: Hazelden Publishing, 2010.

Emiliozzi, Suzie. *Breakthrough Moments: 5 Step Formula for Getting out of Your Own Way and Having the Life You Love.* Scotts Valley, CA: CreateSpace Publishing, 2015

Quinn, Gary. *Living in the Spiritual Zone.* Deerfield Beach, FL: Health Communications, 2005.

Quinn, Gary. *May the Angels Be with You.* San Diego: Jodere Group, 2003.

Quinn, Gary. *The Yes Frequency.* Scotland, UK: Findhorn Press, 2013.

Richardson, Keith. *The Secret of the Butterfly Lovers.* San Francisco: Red Wheel/Weiser, 2007.

Weiss, Brian. *Many Lives, Many Masters.* New York: Touchstone, 1988.